BEEN THERE, DONE THAT, REALLY!

By Paulette Camnetar Meeks

Xulon PRESS

Affirmations

We sometimes forget the elderly, like the folks who have shared their memories in *Been There, Done That, Really!* Their stories bring sadness, laughter and joy. If we only take time to listen, we will learn so much about them, the treasures they hold within and about ourselves.

–Marvin L. Corbitt, Home-Bound Ministry, St. Mary Magdalene Church, Humble Texas

A must read for all health care providers....A gentle reminder for us to continue to treat our patients with compassion and dignity. They are people with wonderful histories as well as our patients.

–Janet Lynne Hartwell, LVN, nineteen years serving in Long-term Nursing Care Humble, Texas

This collection of captivating memories shared is a must read for young and old. These stories tell of the depth and goodness in the elderly among us. Insight and wisdom can be learned from their recorded stories.

–Pat Allcorn, AD
Activities Director for the Elderly in
Long-term Care
Humble, Texas

In this collection of short stories, Paulette Meeks has captured the best of times and, for some, the worst of times. Through their words you can peer into life's many experiences and almost feel the journey from unimagined despair to overwhelming joy. Your spirit will decipher the devastating circumstances these folks lived through, but you will also see the unmistakable hand of a faithful God leading them from tragedy to triumph.

"The memory of the righteous is blessed." (Proverbs 10: 7)

–Pastor Keith Cistrunk, Pastor and Director of Member Care, Grace Church of Humble, Texas

Foreword

While visiting with the elderly, I along with countless others, have heard the statement, "I have lived a lifetime." Although we hear it being said and we feel the depth of the meaning behind it, we all too often neglect, not only the phrase, but the speaker of those words. We rush through the conversations and we move on. We forget. We go about our day, enjoying our own life, never knowing that we've missed something beautiful and irreproducible.

A lifetime is such a gift, full of beauty, soaked in experiences, saturated with lessons learned, hardships had, and miracles and joys encountered. It's full of family and full of friends, full of tears, laughs and blessed with stories. Many tell their stories. Many are unable to tell theirs and many long to tell theirs to someone who will listen. Paulette Meeks gives that listening ear to family, friends and many others who've quietly kept stories in their memories, as she attempts to give a voice to a voiceless generation.

The contributors of this book are "warriors," some still treasured as such, others forgotten in the shuffle of life. Though many are not strong in body, they are pillars of faith and love, strong and steady with experiences to be told and with a lifetime of treasures to share. Reading through their entries, I found myself laughing and relating to them, in more ways than one.

Each person has a life as no other. Each has made and continues to make a mark unable to be copied. Each one's life has great meaning. Each is valuable and has purpose in God's plan and adds to our own.

As you read through these pages, silently listen. You will be blessed by what you hear, a lifetime lived, testimonies and memories gratefully shared in families, in churches, many others forgotten in the dark. The fabric of these lives are remembered and recorded in the light by this heartfelt work of Paulette Camnetar Meeks, *Been There, Done That, Really!*

–Merle Aaron City Councilman, Humble, Texas Deacon, Humble Area First Baptist Church, Humble, Texas

Acknowledgements

With sincere admiration I want to thank my family and many friends for their part in making this book a reality. May God richly bless each one for the memories they've shared. Without their humble telling of these stories, their wisdom and grace could be lost by many having "eyes and see not …and ears and hear not" (Jeremiah 5: 21).

Each story was shared as a blessing and it is my prayer that the blessing continues as these stories touch your life and the lives of those around you. I have learned that many of the elderly have such stories on the "inside" and cannot share them on the "outside" and that those who are able to share, often depend on us for reasons to remember with a smile that they have "**been there and done that, really!**"

With deep gratitude, I want to acknowledge one contributor in "Memorium," Mrs. Ellinor Nieto, whom God called Home in December of 2012. This sweet friend was the first to allow me to record her stories. She wanted the world to hear what a wonderful life God had given her. Her journey, shared so humbly, became the seed He used to blossom into this book. Her stories reflect her faith, hope and love and gave me a glimpse into a soul so ready to begin her wonderful new stories with Jesus in Heaven. Thank you, Ellinor. I love you!

Dedication

This book is dedicated to my grandmother, Helena Berdou, because she was such a wise and loving grandma. It is also dedicated to my beloved husband William David Meeks who made me laugh every time he'd say, "Been there, done that..." Even from heaven these two forever friends have their input in ***Been There, Done That, Really!***

Table of Contents

Grandpa's Horse and Me

—Ellinor Nieto

Coco-Max was my grandfather's horse. He was beige and beautiful. On Sundays, Grandpa would hook him up to a lovely black open carriage. Then, he and I would go for a ride. Coco-Max was so tame. I could hold his reins when I was only four years old. That horse really liked me and he only let us, Grandpa and me feed him.

One summer my grandfather and grandmother went on a vacation for two weeks. Two aunts came to our home to take care of me while my grandparents were away. My uncle who had been injured in the war came with them, so they took care of him and me. But, grandpa's horse – that was a different story.

Coco-Max would not let my aunts get near him. They could not even go into his stable while he was there. When they would try to come near him, he would let them know he didn't want them around. They really were afraid of him.

I would take the buckets of food and crawl under the horse's belly for them and bring his food to the side of the stable where he could eat. I would brush Coco-Max and clean the stable. He let me do everything. He was like a little kitten for me. To exercise him, I would tie him with a rope and walk him around in the yard.

One day I had an idea. I told my aunts while I was exercising Coco-Max they could help by cleaning his stable. I was little and I was smart. I told them it would be nice to either clean the stable or feed Coco-Max. I was too little to do all the work by myself. They chose to clean the stable so my job became fun and wasn't so hard any more. They would say to me, "No, no. We'll clean up the stable."

When, my grandmother and grandfather came back from vacation they asked, "Was everything okay?" My aunts didn't say much other then, "Yes! Everything went fine." My uncle looked at them and wanted to say something. I shook my head at him because I didn't want my grandparents to get upset. I knew my aunts had done their best and I knew I had done a good job, too.

During the weeks that followed, my grandfather let me help him in the garden. We'd take Coco-Max with us as we picked the vegetables and loaded them on him. Coco-Max liked it when I gave him carrots right from the garden. My grandfather and I were very close and Coco-Max

was part of our closeness. He was
like family to us.

*"A righteous man regards the life of
his animal." (Proverbs 12:10)*

Beth and Bill's dog Lucy.

Lucy's Aroma of Protection

– Beth Davidson

L ucy is our sweet ten-year-old pointer mix. She has been our pet for a long time bringing us much joy. It's nice having her because she is good with everyone. Even when the grandchildren were small, she was gentle with them.

Lucy's one big problem is she chases other animals and she tolerates no intruders. When other dogs or cats get into our yard their lives are in danger. It is her yard and she definitely has taken its protection seriously.

One time we heard her barking loudly, so we went outside to find she had trapped the gas meter man into a corner. She was always good to people so we were surprised. We learned though from the man himself that it was his fault. You see, Lucy has a great memory and the man let us know he had kicked at her once before. More than likely she remembered that and it wasn't going to happen again if she could help it. This time we came to the man's rescue and Lucy's, too. No kick or bite happened that day.

Lucy likes sleeping in bed with us and usually stays asleep until we are up and about. One morning she got up very early around 4:30 a.m. and went outside using the doggie door. She was out there for some time. When she came back in, so did a distinct smell. It was truly awful.

It seems an animal had the nerve to trespass into her yard and she didn't like it. She took care of that animal and that visitor took care of her. When she returned to our bed, we could hardly breathe. The smell was so bad. We knew without a second thought that she had a serious encounter with –a – skunk. We jumped up immediately and started to clear the atmosphere.

You can imagine — there were pieces of skunk everywhere and the smell was throughout the house. Let me tell you what I learned. Ketchup and all the tomato sauce in the world does not get rid of that smell. It's just a waste of time and so are a lot of other so-called remedies. We had our work cut out and Lucy had many bath regimes to endure. Finally, with a combination of Dawn and peroxide, she started to smell like our sweet Lucy again.

The next day, the neighbors found five baby skunks under their shed. We were glad they found them before those babies found our protective curious pooch or visa-versa. With her great memory, we are thinking though she learned her lesson and that she will probably go another way if she ever does see such a black and white *cat* again.

"Wash me, and I shall be whiter than snow." (Psalm 51:7)

A Knack for Mischief

– Lois Grahm

I was raised when times were hard. We all had to work. When I was young I washed and ironed clothes, worked in the field, fed the chickens and milked cows. I don't remember how old I was when I milked the first cow. I do remember it wasn't so easy, but I learned. We didn't have a store near our home so nearly everything we had was grown or made at home.

My brother was a year older than I and together we always managed to get into trouble. I also had a half-brother and sister. They were about ten years older. My mother had married before and her husband, their dad, had gotten killed. In fact, he had died in a train accident when my sister was just a year old. My mother met and married my dad ten years later.

My brother and I were very close. We were almost like twins. We went to a little country school. It was a one room school house. We walked about two miles to school every day and walked back home every evening. It's the only way we could get there unless my daddy was going somewhere with his team and wagon. Then, we'd get a ride with him. That didn't happen very often, though.

Our school house was used as a church, too. Whenever a preacher would come through our little town he'd preach there. We'd all go. The denomination of the service didn't matter. When there was a preacher almost the whole town would go to church. It was a special family occasion for us and our neighbors.

I am eighty-four years old now and everyone says I look very young. Maybe, that is because I worked hard all of my life. I didn't use creams on my face and hands. I didn't have time for that. Even after

I married, I worked hard to send my own two boys to school. I took care of our garden, canned vegetables, fruits, etc. I didn't do all the work, but I did a lot. We didn't have freezers in those days; I had to learn to process foods so they would last a long time for us.

We grew peas, corn, green beans, tomatoes, potatoes, squash, cucumbers, peaches, pears and figs. Our place was in Nacogdoches, Texas. Growing up on a farm taught me many skills. It was fun and good hard work. When I was a little girl and my mother would be away from the house, her mother, my grandmother would take care of us.

My brother and I had a knack for getting into mischief. I remember how we tricked Grandma one day when my daddy and older brother were out in the field plowing. My brother and I wanted to go outside so badly and Grandma just wouldn't let us. She was cooking dinner for everyone. Back then the flour and cornmeal were kept in barrels in a storage pantry room at the end of the kitchen. There was a door to the pantry and a lock was put up high, probably so we couldn't reach it. We knew that she would have to go into that room to get what she needed to make the bread for the meal. So, we got us a chair and put it next to the door. We left it setting there.

She probably knew what we were doing and chose not to interfere with our plans.

Grandma finally went in to get the meal she needed to make the bread. We climbed up on that chair, pulled the latch and locked her in. Then, we took off for the fields to where our dad was working. When we got to Daddy he asked us, "Where's Grandma? What's Grandma doing?" We just said, "She's at the house." He didn't think much of it and he didn't ask us anymore.

A little while later, Daddy noticed that there was no smoke coming out of the chimney. So, we all went back to the house. Daddy found Grandma locked in that little room and asked her why she didn't try to call for help. She said she didn't see any need to. All of her quilt scraps were in there and she just sat down and did some of her quilting. She didn't seem to mind. I don't think we even got a spanking for that prank.

One time, we had an old hen that kept on setting and hatching eggs. My folks didn't want her to set any more. They didn't want her to hatch more baby chicks. Someone put a rope or string on her leg so she couldn't fly up to the nest. My brother and I were again into mischief. We went out and turned that chicken loose. Grandma whipped us for that one. She whipped my brother first. He ran by me and said, "Holler real loud and she won't hit you so hard." So I knew what to do. We were *pistols* for sure.

In my home on the farm we had no TV or radio. My dad got a newspaper once in a while, just a little paper with some news on it. Somebody in the neighborhood had a radio and sometimes on a Saturday night we'd go over there and listen to the Grand Old Opry. We made up our own games and enjoyed ourselves outside.

Once, my brother rolled me around in a mud hole. The mud was red. I think he was pretending he was cleaning a hog. It took my mother a week to get all that red clay out of my hair. We were a pair to handle.

There were some cousins close to our age who would come and play with us at times. We were never at a loss making up games and having fun. We played marbles, pick- up sticks and made balls out of unraveled socks and old cut inner-tubes.

We had a dog named "Spot." My brother and I trained him to bring wood in for our stove. We had been over to visit my daddy's parents and my grandpa there showed us how he taught his dog to bring wood in. We figured if Grandpa could do that, we could, too. We went home and started teaching our dog to bring the wood to the back door. He learned quickly and would help us. Spot would bring his pan for food to the back door, too. If we didn't feed him, he'd start beating on the back door with his foot. Lots of times he'd be out hunting and miss supper time. He'd get back home late and there'd be no supper left for him. He'd go to that back door, beat on it and bark until food was put in that pan. He was hungry and he was smart. He not only learned the tricks we taught him, he learned to be like my brother and me and teach us a few of his own.

"Oh, that men would give thanks to the Lord for His goodness, And for His wonderful works to the children of men!" (Psalm 107:31)

Uninvited Guest

— Sanny Laxton

M y mom taught me many lessons as I was growing up. Her bravery came through in many of those lessons. Once she was showing me how to get the eggs from under the chickens in the chicken coop. We went into the coop and she was just about to reach into a nest when a snake slithered near the wall. Those big chicken snakes would come around looking for the eggs just like we did.

Mom was looking at me. She didn't see the snake. I did. I yelled at her to stop. My mom at first didn't know why I was yelling. Then she saw that ugly snake. It was no problem for my mom. She just got a stick and started beating that snake to death. It didn't scare her at all. And, we got to have that egg. Too bad for the snake! He just was not invited to eat our eggs.

Out in the country I learned many lessons. I was only about three years old at the time. There were always new things for me to learn and being careful because of the snakes was just one of them.

There was a company near us that had a water faucet connected to its building. We didn't have running water at that time. Neither did our neighbors. The company would let us draw the water we needed from their faucet. My mom and the neighbor lady would go together to get water.

My uncle, my brother and I would go along with my mom. We would have to walk through a cow pasture to get to the water. My uncle and both of us kids would pick up the dry cow pies, put them in buckets and take them home for our garden. Those cow pies didn't smell good, but they surely made our garden grow and our fresh home-grown food always smelled good. We were learning very quickly tricks of good farming.

We always had vegetables growing like tomatoes, potatoes, corn, green beans, lettuce, cucumbers and squash. We grew strawberries, too. My grandpa even had a huge watermelon farm.

We had a cow for a short while. Mom was taking care of it for a neighbor who needed to go out of town for a time. Once while Mom was staking it out in the field, I was with her and that cow locked her horn in my dress and threw me into the air. After that, Mom didn't keep that cow any longer than she needed. She did get milk from her for a while but because of what she did to me, she was not welcomed again as a guest on our farm. And, to this day, I am still scared of cows. I won't go near them. We did get some little goats for milking after that. They were gentle, not a bit like that cow.

During those days my brother and I played in the woods near our home. We'd find long vines in the trees and swing from them like monkeys. We loved this and could swing high and far. We also would go pick blackberries. When pine nuts fell we'd gather them and Daddy would use them to make a fire for cooking. Those pine nuts made our food taste so delicious.

At bath time, I always wanted to be first. You know why? We all used the same water. When you were first, the water was clean and warm.

When you were last, guess what? It was dirty and cold. Who wants a dirty cold bath? I didn't. And besides, you can guess what my brother did in his bath water. One time he wanted to be first. I cried because I didn't want to be after him. I thought I would get dirty from that bath since he had just been playing in the dirt.

We lived near a creek. We'd go with our daddy and walk down to that creek. He'd hunt for squirrels and rabbits. After the hunting, we'd all go fishing in that creek.

We didn't have a school in Clover Leaf where we lived so we rode a school bus and went to school in another town. The bus was so crowded because children from all over went to that one school. The first day we arrived at school we were all finger printed. At that time there was such a bomb scare. I guess they figured finger printing was the best identification if something terrible happened. The Texaco Refinery was right there by the school, so the town people probably thought where we lived would be a likely target if the USA would be hit by a bomb sent to our country. Our drive to school was right through the refinery and the storage tanks. That probably was also the reason for the many bomb shelter drills at our school. Bomb shelters were all over and plans for safety were frequently talked about. We all knew what to do and where to go in an emergency.

My teacher's house was right next to the refinery. Once she took us on a field trip and we even got to see the inside of her house. She was an old lady. In those days when the ladies her age dyed their hair, it usually had a light blue shade to it. But my teacher, her hair was lavender purple. I was in first grade. It was 1942. I don't remember her name, but I do remember her purple hair.

"See that you walk circumspectly, not as fools but as wise…"
(Ephesians 5:15)

Bill and Paulette on wedding day

Never Too Old

to Be Smitten

—Paulette Meeks

Sixty great years I had been given all rich in blessings. I never wanted for anything. I had everything I needed, love of my family and friends, good health, a nice home and grace that kept me busy and so happy working and caring for others. I had just returned home from Mexico. God had always spoiled me as His child there. Even in hovels of the poorest of the poor I felt I belonged and I was always accepted as family and friend. I had always wanted to be with His poorest children and God had so graciously given me my wish. Now, my heart was excited and I didn't know why. I just knew He had something planned for me. I had told my Mexican Sister friends and missionaries as I left them that I would probably not be returning at least for a while. I would go home to the Valley in southern Texas, pray and wait for God's call in my heart. When I knew, I would let them know God's plan for me.

As I was cleaning my home and doing odds and ends around the house and yard, it occurred to me to fiddle around with an old computer a friend had given me. Then the thought came to my heart that I should put a web site out on the internet to find the person God wanted as my partner. What a strange thought! I never felt the need of a partner before, why would I want one now? The truth was that was the farthest thing from my mind. But, I wasn't surprised that God had put such a thought in me. He always did surprise me.

All my life, I wanted to do what God wanted. If this thought was of Him, I would trust Him and I would enjoy this adventure. So, my search began. I was really on foreign ground. I trusted God's way and His reason. I put a web site on the internet saying basically I was searching for a Christian widower. I received too many lonely heart responses. I knew none were God's choice for me. One day I thought of stopping this search. I was getting tired of hearing so many sad stories. Then it happened. I received a one liner from a William David Meeks. I knew the second I received his e-mail, he was the one.

Bill and I met for the first time via that e-mail in the latter part of November, 2000, right before Thanksgiving. We sent many e-mails and finally in January of 2001, we "discovered" our phones. We both were like teens talking all night. We enjoyed learning so much about each other from the inside. What a terrific gift. We were definitely falling in love with each other's souls. I would count the seconds waiting for his phone calls and I bet he did the same for mine.

In April this sweet man invited me to Humble, Texas to help him celebrate a local city event, Good Oil Days. He found a motel, Champions Inn, near his home, for me. I arrived April 19, 2001 to see for the first time my Matchmaker's choice for me. I knew the moment I saw those blue eyes, heard his soft voice, and his Meeks' laugh, he was to be my sweet partner for the rest of my life.

On my birthday, April 20, 2001, we went on our first date, a picnic in Jesse Jones Park. He gave me a "peachy" birthday gift with all kinds of peach-smelling lotions. On that day, he also gave me his special nickname, "Peaches." Good Oil Days followed and walking through the town with him affirmed how proud he was to be a Christian as he introduced me to so many of his brothers and sisters from Grace Church of Humble.

Bill came to the Valley where I lived in May, bringing papers to finalize our plans for marriage. Neither of us ever knew who proposed first or if we ever did propose. We just knew we were meant to walk the rest of our journey hand-in-hand and heart-to-heart to heaven as husband and wife. We were married June 29, 2001, began our honeymoon in Hawaii and continued it for the next six years.

May 23, 2007, Jesus hugged into heaven, my very best friend, my husband, the dearest treasure ever shared with me by God Himself. Though, we were not ready to say good-bye, I definitely never would be. Jesus was calling and I needed to let my precious partner go. It was the saddest good-bye ever. Now, I wait for my hug. I will see the twinkle in my sweet Bill's eye and hear him laugh when we meet again face-to-face in an eternal hello. A friend said, "We never lose those we give to God." And I know that is true. Every moment I had with my sweetheart was a moment of grace. And grace is forever!

"Husbands love your wives just as Christ also loved the church

and gave Himself for her."
(Ephesians 5:25)

Taking Mother's Place

— Dorothy Louise Elder

I was born in 1929 during the Great Depression. My dad went to South America and worked. When work ended there, he came back home. I was quite young with a little brother and a little sister. My mother accidentally drowned in the Sabine River shortly after Daddy came home. Daddy never re-married and I had to learn how to be a mother for my little sister and brother.

Some good friends of my dad moved on the farm to help him out with the farm work. The lady was a help to me. She encouraged me, taught me how to cook and do housework and many things. I was seven years old when I learned to cook, make corn-bread, get up early in the morning and make biscuits for the family.

My grand-daddy had a sugar mill. I would fix breakfast for the family and then go push the sugar-cane through the mill with him. After that I would get ready and help my little brother and sister. Then we would go to school.

When we were in grade school, there was a truck that would come by every morning and pick us up to take us to school. There were seats for each of us in that truck. When we went to high school we had a different routine. High school was about four miles away in a town called Newton. We'd get up very early and take a real school bus there. Daddy didn't want us to miss school and I really didn't want to miss either. I was determined to finish high school. Of course, while we were in school, Daddy worked all day on the farm.

The town I grew up in was Bon Weir, Texas. It was a small town named after two doctors. My grand-daddy built log houses for many people and was well known in town. He built our home, too in Bon Weir. I remember he had many men who worked with him building those houses.

Miss Tilly was the good friend who stood by us and encouraged me to go to beauty school after high school. I don't know what I would have done without her. When I was a young child, she helped me learn to be in charge at home and later taught me to be a beautician. She had a beauty shop and even let me practice in that shop.

One of my aunts sent me tickets when I graduated from high school to go with my little sister to Pasadena California. She wanted me to check out the beauty schools there. We didn't know it at the time but I needed a license to practice my work there. The Texas license wouldn't do. So my ability to work as a beautician was lost in Pasadena. While there, we saw the Rose Parade and many beautiful sites. It was a nice place to rest for a while. After a couple of weeks, we returned home so I could help care for my brother and sister who were still in school.

I have good memories of those days with my sister and brother, my daddy, grand-daddy and those friends who stayed by us, encouraging us to stay in school, learn everything we could, support each other as family and never give up.

Times were hard, but we had enough and we had each other.

"Therefore, since we are receiving a kingdom which cannot be shaken, let us have grace, by which we may serve God accept-ably with reverence and godly fear." (Hebrews 12:28)

Argentina

—Ellinor Nieto

One day my husband said to me, "I have a surprise for you…a beautiful trip to Argentina." I was all excited. Argentina, I hadn't been there, you know. We flew on an Argentine Airline to Buenos Aires. We had a whole day lay-over so I got to go shopping. The stores there had so many beautiful things made of fine leather. I bought a two-piece skirt and jacket and a coat.

My father-in-law left me money when he passed away so I could have almost bought a building there. I had never had anything like that happen to me before. Having money left to me like that really touched me. I spent some of that inheritance and bought nice things from his country, Argentina. That was generous of him to think of me and now I would think of him when I wore those beautiful Argentine leather clothes.

After shopping we went to the train station. There, at 10:00 p.m. we took a train for Rosario the second largest city in Argentina. The trip took about seven hours on this train. They called it the express train. There was no food but they did give us something to drink. We sat up all the way, because in Argentina there were no trains at that time with sleeping quarters.

We arrived in Rosario early in the morning around 7:00. We were the only people who got off the train in Rosario. We carried two heavy suitcases, one with our clothes and necessities and one with gifts for my Argentine in-laws. We had to walk about two and a half miles, my husband with those suitcases and me in high heels. I was ready to *hang* my sweetheart. I was really "giving it to him." I told him, "I'll never forget you for this." He did feel badly about this part of the trip.

We finally arrived at the house. It was such a strange house. We had to walk up many stairs and then there was a door. The house was not like houses I was used to. Hector told me to knock on the door. When I did, the door opened into a bedroom. This was most unusual to me. Soon, some of his family came into that room and warmly greeted us. His mother embraced me so tightly. They were so very excited to see us.

Then, they took us into the living room where I met the whole family. There were about ten different cousins speaking in Spanish. They all wanted to meet me. They kept talking to me and I just responded with "Si!" the only word I knew. Then they would say, "She speaks Spanish" and were so excited.

Later, four brothers arrived. They all were doctors and had studied English. Finally, someone started speaking to me in English and I understood what was being said. They asked me questions like, "Do you really love our brother?" Of course I said, "Yes!" They asked, "Is he a good guy?" I said, "Yes, he is." They looked surprised. I think they thought no one could possibly love their brother. But I did.

We were then taken out to the patio where a cook had prepared a special meal. Soon this huge meal was placed on the table before us.

They love mayonnaise. Every part of that meal had mayonnaise on it or by it. There were boiled eggs with mayonnaise on top, chicken with mayonnaise on top, something else with mayonnaise on top. I looked at my husband wondering what this was about. He returned my look with his own questioning one. It was so funny. I would eat one egg then immediately someone put another on my plate with more mayonnaise on top. They would put more mayonnaise on my plate and say, "Good, good, good!"

"...Jesus said to him, 'Go home to your friends, and tell them what great things the Lord has done for

*you, and how He has had compas-
sion on you'." (Mark 5:19)*

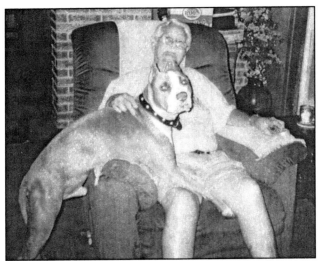

JC rests his paws on his pal Harry.

Comfort Comes A-Leaping

—Joyce Wiggins

I feel secure in my Savior and I feel secure in my salvation. It is great to have these things established in my heart. I am secure in that my husband and family love me and that I have friends who care about me.

We have a pit-bull named JC. He weighs nearly eighty pounds. He's been loved all of his life and he is a big baby. When we let him outside, he wants us to go with him. We open the door and he goes out, then looks back waiting for us to go, too. If we close the door, he just stays there and barks.

I went outside with him this morning and he had the best time chasing squirrels and birds. He ran up and down the whole length of the fence barking at the dogs next door. Every once in a while he'd look back to see if one of us was on the porch. If we go in, here he comes. I don't know if he's just a big spoiled dog, or if he's just insecure being outside alone.

Oh well, we love him and want him to be secure. Thank God we never have to feel so insecure in our relationship with Jesus. We don't have to look back and wonder like JC. Jesus says He'll never leave us or forsake us. This promise has always meant a lot to me. Jesus has always been there for me in every trial and I love Him.

There were times when I said, "God, where are You?" In my heart I knew He was close by. He is always faithful. Praise God!

We love our big baby JC and want him to know we will always be there for him and he is secure with us. We will probably keep on going outside with him just so he feels safe, just like God is our security when we go out and when we stay in.

What a wonderful Savior we have. I felt secure in His comfort when my precious husband Harry was sick. After we came home from the hospital, Harry needed help getting from his wheelchair to his easy chair. To prepare for this, I had to put JC in the yard while I helped Harry get comfortable. Harry was weak and I didn't want JC to try to knock either of us down in his exuberance.

After Harry was comfortable resting in his easy chair, I let JC back in the house. Our sweet pet didn't know what was going on. He had two things on his mind: he was afraid of being alone in the yard and he missed Harry for too long. He probably figured all was well and back to normal. He just needed to add a little more comfort to the scene.

As I opened the back door to let him in, you can guess what happened. Our pup had one aim and it was Harry. The wait had been too long for him. This big baby of ours, all eighty pounds of him, took one flying leap, landed on Harry's stomach and welcomed him home. Even though my Harry was out of breath from this comfort-giving pup, he welcomed such adoring comfort with a painful, but still loving smile.

"Therefore if there is any con-solation in Christ, if any comfort of love… fulfill my joy by being likeminded…" (Philippians 2:1-2)

Treasures in Travels

-- Mary Gene Hortman

I have traveled a lot. My husband was in the Army and was stationed in Hawaii. When I was newly married, we lived there on the Island of Oahu for fifteen months. My first son was born at the Army hospital in Honolulu. Living in Hawaii was one of the happiest times in my life. This Island is such a special place with so many good memories. Maybe the island has changed now, but, I still remember how beautiful it was.

After the Army, my husband worked as a petroleum engineer and because of his job, we traveled overseas to foreign countries. We went to Venezuela with our two sons and our baby daughter. Living this far from Houston was a new experience. This was a poor country. We lived in a little camp. Our house was very nice. I worked as a secretary while my husband did his job with the oil company. One rich experience for me living in Venezuela was I learned Spanish. It was a great opportunity.

The help was not expensive and during the six years there I picked up a lot of Spanish. I appreciated the chance to learn. For me it was wonderful. My boys were in school and my baby girl had a nanny who spoke Spanish. The people there made it easy to learn their language.

The mountains were in driving distance for us and we would take family trips there. The view was beautiful and the air was so crisp and clear. The place where we lived was called, *"Las Morochas"* which in Spanish there means *"the twins."* After six years, we came back home to Houston, Texas having had rich experiences, new found friends and for me, the ability to understand and speak Spanish.

The thing that I found so interesting and surprising was people are the same wherever you go. They could have been unkind to Americans because a lot of what Americans did really was foreign to them; even not acceptable to their own way of life. But, these people always were welcoming, friendly and outgoing to us. Venezuela was especially warm to Americans. We were always free to be ourselves. It was my experience that we were never treated as strangers, but rather as friends and neighbors.

Later, because of my husband's job, we traveled again, this time to Libya, an Arab country, with very different experiences. Here we lived in Tripoli. I didn't learn the Arabic language. It was very difficult. The country was under Gaddafi. He was nice to the Americans at that time because our work in the oil industry was so important to him and to Libya.

Even though we didn't speak each other's language, I have nice memories. Everyone was kind to us in many ways. Though many of our customs they did not do, they respected us with our differences. They accepted us with our parties, alcohol, sun bathing ...so many activities not allowed to them. They welcomed us warmly. We lived there for three years.

The *"guiblis,"* that's what the natives called *the sandstorms*, were frightening. Our husbands worked away often far in the desert area. The wives and children were alone at night when the sandstorms would usually come. I remember the noise and the fear I felt surrounded by those *"guiblis."* All the windows in our home had to be covered during these storms. The sound of the rushing sands could be deafening and the darkness made it worse. It was eerie. No one could go out because the sand was so thick. Looking at the windows, I would only see the covering and it was just blackness. The sand would be pounding on the window coverings and on the whole house. I was glad for quiet nights.

Our next journey took us to Iran. The Shah was in power there at the time. He was well liked but there were rumors of threats to his life, so people were not allowed to get too close to him. Once, the Shah was passing near our house. I was fortunate because my house was two houses down from the highway. The "house boy" an employee who helped us with chores around the house, went with me up on our roof and we got to watch the entourage pass by. We considered the Shah a good friend. It was a thrill to see him as he went by in that open car.

Another incident I remember well was a particular visit to a pharmacy in Ahwaz, Iran. While I was there another customer, through an interpreter, since neither of us understood each other's language, invited me to her home for coffee. It touched me that this total stranger would be so thoughtful to open her home to me through this act of kindness. I remember that thoughtfulness to this very day. There were no boundaries that separated us.

I am grateful for my experience living in lands far away, seeing so much beauty all over the world and especially in meeting so many people of different cultures. The most important lesson I have learned through my many travels is that our likenesses are greater than our differences. The differences you can see, hear, and touch. The likenesses are deeper and make us who we are wherever we are.

"I drew them with gentle cords, with bands of love. And I was to them as those who take the yoke from their neck." (Hosea 11:4)

Volunteer Mom

— Sanny Laxton

In Michigan, at the Air Force base, I went to sign my daughter up in a Brownie Troop. Little did I know what this year held for me! I became her troop leader. Then I went to my first parent-teacher conference and left as the room mother. My son went to school and came home telling me he volunteered me to help his class. My husband came with more news to keep me busy; I was to be his friend's assistant Junior/Cadet Troop leader. This was going to be a very active and interesting year.

My camping experience with my own family came to the rescue. When the Junior/Cadets went on their first hiking experience, they got lost in the wilderness. I knew how to find my way out. I told the leader to follow the creek and it would lead to the highway. She was grateful because that bit of knowledge really did get us back to civilization.

All of these volunteer activities kept me busy and kept me learning. The Junior Leader encouraged me to teach the little ones a lot about camping. We didn't stay in over-night camp-outs, but everyone learned important camping jobs to do. I wanted them to be ready to step up when it was their time to become Junior/Cadets. They had many skills to learn and I had to learn them first. We carried water to be sure we were fire-safe. We cooked hot dogs and toasted marshmallows. We learned safety for ourselves and others. I even taught them to bake cookies. We baked so many cookies one time that we brought some to a local orphanage.

When I helped with the Junior/Cadet Troop we did stay over-night at the camps. We had to stay in tents in the wilderness. One of the husbands would stay out of the camp, but near enough to protect us in case bears, etc. came around. The girls would put their food in pots in the ground and cover them with coals so they would cook. They would have to tie their food up high in trees so bears wouldn't be tempted to come. Food that had to be kept cool would be put in jars and tied to a string, then put in the river. The water would keep the food inside cool.

One Junior/Cadet was working on her Silver Award. We had to go deep into the center of the woods, sit around a camp fire, sing songs, try to not freeze, and wait for the Cadet to find us. It took hours and we were beginning to worry, but it was worth the wait. She did find us. And we would soon be ready to celebrate.

The next day we had the ceremony for the girls to all step up to the next level. Parents were invited. We had the wood really high because of the fire we needed to build. A wind came up and the wood fell causing the fire to spread. We quickly formed a water brigade that extended from the river to the wood. All the parents passed buckets of water to put out the fire. Without the parents we could have had a real forest fire. This made for a very appreciative and exciting ceremony. I still remember it and I bet the girls and their parents do, too.

During those days I often drove our twenty-five foot motor home with my troop of Junior/Cadets in tow to different activities. Every Saturday during winter I was their chauffeur to and from swimming lessons. The trip to the pool was about twenty miles away. The pool was indoors in a school. All the girls were excited and learned to swim. The last Saturday as it was time to return home, snow flurries fell. My companion leader wanted to stay and shop in town. I decided to go ahead and take the girls home.

The snow started to fall harder and there were snow drifts on the road. I thought I would get stuck in snow drifts along the way. Everything went smoothly until I needed to slow down and exit to the left. My brakes wouldn't work. I couldn't slow down.

Finally the brakes did work and my camper turned completely around and we were going back up the exit ramp. It was scary but we remained safe and finally parked slowly on the side of the road. I called my friends and we stayed put until help came to take us back home. I was grateful that we made the trip back. My friend, who stayed to shop, was snow-bound and couldn't come home. The girls and I, with stubborn brakes, snow drifts, screams and scary moments got home safe and secure. God had His Hand on us and He didn't let us go.

"God is our refuge and strength,
A very present help in trouble."
(Psalm 46:1)

Perry Como, Ellen and baby Mike

My Singing Friend

—*Ellen Camnetar*

E ven as a young child I loved a singer named Perry Como. His songs were beautiful. To me, they were the best and he was the best singer. Every time a new song of his came out, I learned it. I probably remember every one of his songs even to this day. I also have just about all of his records.

I started my own Perry Como fan club. We probably had about five members. That was alright with Mr. Como. He recognized me and his secretary was quick to send me tickets whenever he would come to New Orleans. He was important, a real professional artist. As great as he was, he was equally humble. He didn't put himself above others. I know this from my own experience.

Though I was just an ordinary young girl, he let me know I was important to him. When Perry Como came to New Orleans for the Kraft Music Hall, his secretary told me where he'd be staying. I went to his room in the hotel and was warmly greeted by his brother-in-law and by Mr. Como at his door. He graciously greeted me letting me know he was pleased to see me. He told me that anytime he would be in New Orleans, my home town, I would have an invitation to visit him. My sister Annette was waiting downstairs in the car for me, hoping not to get a ticket or get arrested for double parking, so this first visit was short but warm as Perry Como, my star, greeted me making me feel like I was his official New Orleans Ambassador.

In 1976, Perry Como was King of Bacchus for the Mardi Gras Parade. I got to watch him as he was escorted royally down the parade route. He sent me a message that later I was invited to be with him on the river boat, the Natchez. This is a very beautiful paddle boat that goes down the Mississippi River. I was excited about that invitation and took my son Michael with me. I could see Perry Como on the boat as he was motioning for me to come on. The policeman at the gate wasn't letting me on because I didn't have a ticket. He looked up and when Perry motioned, he let me go aboard with my son. I was so excited. My little son Michael and I were on the Natchez with my favorite singer in the whole world, Perry Como.

As I sat at a table with Perry glowing with all my heart for such an honor, my son Michael was not enthralled at all. He started crying. He was only about three years old and had no idea who this stranger was. Perry Como stayed so calm. He picked up my sweet baby boy, put him on his lap and started singing to him. Michael quieted down very quickly. I think he became at that moment Perry Como's newest and youngest fan.

Perry Como didn't know much about New Orleans cuisine. He was eating red beans and rice and asked me why someone would put beans over the rice. He thought that was a good way to ruin good food. I explained that it is really the only way to eat red beans and rice for it to be, oh so good, the way it is meant to be.

Perry Como was not just an artist who sang, he treated people with kindness and hope. He didn't just sing those meaningful songs. He lived the lyrics in the songs he sang. He didn't let his importance as a singing artist take away from his humility and grace. Though I was very young when I first met him, he always treated me with acceptance and sincere respect. Even now that I am much older, I can still say Perry Como is the best. His songs are the best. And I am blessed to have known him as my friend.

"He…set my feet upon a rock, And established my steps. He has put a new song in my mouth— Praise to our God." (Psalm 40:2-3)

My Grandmother's Farm

– Elizabeth Marshall

I am proud to be a grandmother and a great-grandmother. I just celebrated my ninety-first birthday this past week and still remember my grandmother on my father's side. By sharing my memories I hope to give the youngest members of my family a chance to know their great-great- grandmother. Well, let me tell you about her.

The parents of Elsie Prescott, my mother, I never knew. I vaguely remember seeing my grandmother on Mom's side once. Mom took my three sisters and me to Michigan to visit her. I was very little and don't remember much about that visit. My father was John Prescott and his mother, I knew very well because I grew up on her farm in Enon Valley, Pennsylvania.

Both my grandfather and my grandmother on my dad's side came from England. My grandmother, Mary Garner, came to America with two children. She was married in England and her husband died. Mary settled in Pittsburgh with her two children, Jenny and Edward and opened a boarding house. My grandfather, John Prescott, was one of her first boarders. They quickly fell in love and married. Their story continued when my grandmother bought a ninety-six acre farm in Pennsylvania. I know she is the one who bought it and for definite, since I grew up there, I can say, she ruled that roost.

After my grandparents married, they had my father, John Thomas, in 1884 and a daughter Blanche. Blanche married and had two little girls. Later she became sick with the flu and died in 1918. The girls grew up with their father and their Aunt Lizzie who often stepped in to help him. They spent summers with us on the farm.

Our farm was about five miles from the railroad tracks and during the Depression, so many men who were down and out (they called them hobos in those days) would come to the farm for handouts. My mother always fed them. She'd have them sit on the back porch and bring them something she'd cook for them. Then they'd go on their way again.

Those days during the Depression were so terrible. Times were hard on everyone. Ruth, my oldest sister married around 1930. She and her husband and their five children stayed at the farm until times were better. My parents helped them get their own place.

My grandmother's farm was always a happy and busy place. I've often wondered how my mother and father survived and my grandmother, too. What hard work they must have done to manage caring for us and for so many others. The farm was always a place of welcome.

Grandma's farm had a huge barn and a farmhouse with a kitchen, a dining room, and five bedrooms. There was heat in just the kitchen and the dining room. The rest of the house was cold. In the winter it was actually freezing in most of those rooms.

When I was a child, I was told the house was a hundred years old. Just last winter I had turned the

TV on around five in the morning. I had never done that before. This morning I don't know why, I just decided to look at the news. The newscaster announced there had been a house fire in Enon Valley. I thought, "I'll bet it's our farmhouse, the old place where I was born." It was. It had burned to the ground.

So, the farm that Mary Garner Prescott bought, the place that was home to me for so long is gone. That news made me sad. But the memories I have of that farm will never be gone...good memories of growing up; getting to really know my grandmother and her generosity in letting us share in what was hers in the hardest of times; and helping so many others, too, never counting the cost, always giving more. This memory lives on in me and I hope it will in my children, my grandchildren and my great-grandchildren.

"But do not forget to do good and to share, for with such sacrifices God is well pleased." (Hebrews 13:16)

Yes, Everything

—Ellinor Nieto

I was born in Lower Saxony, Germany on September 10, 1936. It was not safe in my hometown because of the war. My father had been killed before I was born. When I was seven days old, my mother took me and we moved to be with my grandparents. My mother worked in a factory and my grandparents took care of me during the day.

My girlfriend Helga and I were like sisters. Every place we went, we went together. One day when I was seven years old, we were both walking my dog and all of a sudden my dog ran as fast as he could back home. Then we heard a sound. It was an airplane, a bomber plane. It flew very low. It was so close we could even see the pilot. That is the first time I ever saw a black man. It was one of the planes of the Tuskegee Squadron Fighter pilots.

My dog already had sensed something was to be feared. We realized it was dangerous and we both ran back home. We went into the cellar. One of those incendiary bombs hit our house. It landed right in my bedroom on my pillow. Everything there was burning. It didn't hurt us because we were safe in the cellar. Had this happened at night, I would have been asleep in that bed. God took care of me. I was so young, but even at that age I knew He had kept me safe.

My grandpa went up to put out the fire in my bedroom. His head got burned badly. I went up to help. He said, "Child you shouldn't be here!" I was stubborn and wouldn't leave. I wanted to help him. I said, "What can I do?" He said throw everything you can out of the window. I had many collections of books and I threw all of them out the window as my grandpa had told me. I asked my grandpa again, "Do I throw everything out of the window?" He said, "Everything, everything!"

I grabbed the chamber pot and asked him again, "Do I throw out everything through the window?" He said again, "Everything, everything!" So I got the chamber pot which was made of porcelain and was beautiful. It was not quite empty from the night before and I threw it out the window. Next thing I heard was a very loud, "Ouch!" My neighbor was helping outside and you can guess what happened. The chamber pot with all its contents hit him directly on the head.

My neighbor didn't talk to me for weeks. He didn't even say a word to me until the bump on his head had disappeared. My grandpa, in the meantime, went to the store that had made the first chamber pot and had another made. This new one even had my name put on it."

"I will both lie down in peace, and sleep For You alone, O Lord, make me dwell in safety." (Psalm 4:8)

Beth and little sister Cynthia all dressed up.

A Girl Grows Up

– Beth Davidson

I grew up in Enon Valley, Pennsylvania. I was the second of four children of a great mom and dad. My father was a welder by profession, but he knew how to do just about anything. My mother was a homemaker but was always busy about many other things, too.

There were no other little girls around my neighborhood and since it was a farming community, I didn't wear girly things. I liked to play with my brothers and the other boys. I enjoyed being outside, in the barn, playing ball, running through the woods or anything else my friends were up to at the time.

Though my mother was an excellent seamstress, my first grade school outfits were nice jeans and white sweaters and that is what I liked. Back in those days you'd find me climbing a tree before you'd see me with a baby doll.

When I was nine and a half, my little sister was born. She was really girly and so cute and smart. At that time I probably took on more of a girl's role in my family because of her. I began to appreciate pretty dresses and my mom sewed me many, all the way through my high school years and even when I was a young adult. My dresses were perfect and no one ever had any as beautiful as mine.

We lived in an Amish area and sometimes young Amish boys would join my brothers in the fields. When I was about fourteen years old, an Amish boy in the neighborhood took an interest in me. I could tell he really liked me. It was against his religion to come into our house. After church on Sunday afternoons, he'd come anyway, park his horse and buggy behind our house, come in, sit in my father's chair and watch television. He told me he really liked me and wanted to buy me dishes and things for our wedding. That never happened. Probably my dad and mom had a lot to do with that plan not becoming a reality.

I was allowed to date and most of the boys I did date were from church. We'd often go to the bowling alley where my dad was a chaperone. One night my date drove me there and when we were ready to bowl, he realized he had forgotten his wallet at home. My dad paid for our date that night.

Another memory that is so fresh today is how I learned to drive. I was about sixteen and I learned on an old international harvester tractor and in an old international truck. I wasn't sure I would ever learn to drive with that standard shift, but I mastered it and passed my driving test. I also learned to bale hay and combine wheat. Those were great experiences. Since we lived in farm country and our friends had farms, these were jobs common to most teens then. These were the vehicles used by most also except for the Amish with their horses and buggies.

My memories of family, friends, church and community keep me smiling even today.

"To everything there is a season, a time for every purpose under heaven… a time to plant and a time to pluck what is planted…"
(Ecclesiastes 3:1-2)

A Drop in the Bucket

–Joyce Wiggins

There are times when we are in prayer and have our minds on the Lord and God talks to us. This happened to me. I was thanking Him for His love and His goodness and His mercy to my sweet husband Harry and me. I prayed, "Lord, we still want to be useful to the Kingdom of God. I know we're not much, like a drop in a bucket. He is eighty-four and I am eighty-two." God stopped me from going on. He said to me, "Every drop is important to Me."

Isn't that something? Isn't God good? We are all important to Him. We are all important to His Kingdom. Maybe we can't teach, say wonderful prayers, sing or play an instrument, but there are times when a smile, a hug, or a handshake does a world of good.

I hope that I have dropped something into your heart today to let you know you are important to God. He cares. He always cares. In our minds we can't imagine the love of God. He loves the Christians who love Him but He also loves those who hate Him. He's always standing with open arms for anyone who will come to Him. Oh what a Savior!

Your little drop in the bucket and my little drop in the bucket are important to God. No telling what we can accomplish if we put all our drops together. We could cause a flood. We can and we will see healings as never before, see lonely and broken hearts mended by our efforts. Praise God! I know He has a use for every one of us.

"And we know that all things work together for good to those who love God, to those who are the called according to His purpose..."
(Romans 8:28)

My Little Lamb

—Leslie Ann Stretch

When I was twelve and my brother was nine, one day during the summer we were really bored. On this particular day City Park in New Orleans had a grand opening for its petting zoo. We lived very near the park and my grandmother suggested that the both of us go have a good time there. She gave us whatever money we needed, a quarter or more for our tickets and away we went.

One person's ticket would win the grand prize. They had an opening ceremony and we saw all the animals there: the ducks, chickens, geese, goats, pigs, lambs. All of the animals had their own story line. I remember one of the animals had a big old shoe by it. There was even a whale that we went into. Inside we saw all kinds of fish. The animals at the petting zoo were small and friendly. We did have fun at that grand opening.

They announced they were going to draw for the grand prize. I tried to convince my brother that we could share with each other if one of us won. I told him, "If I win, we could split it. Or, if you win, we could split it." That way we'd each have half the prize. My brother didn't agree with my suggestion. He just said, "Nope, absolutely not!" He was the lucky one. He would always win, so I guess he thought he would win this time and wanted to keep the whole prize.

We were standing in line waiting for the winner to be picked and what a surprise we had. They picked my number. They had about a hundred people there, but I was the lucky one. The prize was either a five dollar bill or a little lamb. Being twelve years old, of course I picked the lamb. They had a pink ribbon around its neck, but there was no way for me to walk it home. And, it was too heavy for us to carry.

Some lady there offered us a ride home thinking that my parents would object to that lamb and then she would get to keep it. We probably shouldn't have accepted a ride from a stranger, but we really had no other way to get that little lamb home. It was just a couple of blocks away and we needed the help.

I brought the lamb up on the porch and my grandmother came out and said, "Who are those people?" I told her that the lady was just someone who rode us home because I won the grand prize, we needed help getting the lamb home and the lady wanted to take the lamb if we couldn't keep it. My grandmother waved to that lady and said, "Yes!" I could keep the lamb.

We had a big two story house on City Park Avenue with a basement. I got to stake my lamb out on the front lawn during the day and she would sleep in the basement at night. I named her Delilah because we had a German-shepherd named Samson. So now we had a Samson and a Delilah. She was our grass cutter, eating all the grass and the bushes as far as she could reach. An old man who walked by every day gave us a better stake so she could walk even further; it was more secure in the ground and she couldn't get loose.

My mom and grandmother told me I would be responsible for my little lamb. So, I was. I would clean up after her and take her for walks like a dog on a leash. I would even walk her to City Park. It got to the point where I didn't even need the leash. She knew me and would just follow me. She would disappear into a bush and eat weeds around the base of the trees. People would want to take their picture with her. Some people thought she escaped from the petting zoo and tried to catch her. I would often buy her a coke at the concession stand. She liked to eat the ice and drink the coke out of a cup.

My little Delilah was very domesticated. Eventually she got too big and we couldn't keep her at home any more. My mother was head chemist for the state of Louisiana. There were many sheep at the place where she worked. So my lamb went to live with those other sheep. She was different from the rest because she wasn't afraid of people. All the other sheep would huddle together when people came around. Delilah would just walk right up toward the people and let them pet her. When we brought her to meet the others, she jumped in the food bin, sat there and ate all the food. I guess she thought it was all for her. She ate the whole thing. It was a great place for her. She was safe and happy and I would get to visit her often.

One time when I went to visit my little lamb, Delilah had a surprise to show me. There she was with her very own baby lamb. She had a good life and added much to mine. One night Delilah and I became famous. A TV station heard about Delilah and there on the news was our story. The main caption said, "Mary had a little lamb and so did Leslie Ann."

"The Lord is my shepherd, I shall not want. He lets me lie down in green pastures." (Psalm 23:1-2)

Archie checks Sanny's car.

A Dashboard Prayer

—Sanny Laxton

I had a custom of putting my hands on the dashboard when I would get into my car. With both hands resting there I would ask God to protect me and anyone else who would be traveling with me. I wonder how many times God did step in. Once in a while He'd let me know He was there.

After my sister moved to Pearland, Texas, she called and asked me to come see her new house. My brother Archie's two little girls, my nieces, wanted to come with me. I said, "Okay." So, the three of us went down to Pearland for a visit. We had visited quite a while then, before it got dark, I decided we should go back home. My nieces were little and I didn't want to keep them out too late.

We were on 59 South close to Richmond and I said, "Let's get something to eat before we go home. Are you two hungry?" They said, "Yes!" We stopped for hamburgers and milkshakes. We got back in the car and hadn't gone too far when the lights on the car went out. I was in the left lane and had to pull over to the side of the road. I stopped my car and then tried to fool around with the switch to make the lights go back on. I turned around and noticed my two little nieces sound asleep in the back seat of the car. I said, "God, you know I can't carry them back to Wharton and it's getting late. I can't leave them in the car either." I asked Him to please help me. I didn't know what to do. I reminded God that my little nieces and I needed Him right then and there.

I tried again to turn on the lights and immediately they went on. I thanked God because I knew He took care of us when no one else could. I got back home safely and walked the two girls back across the street to their house. I said to Archie, "My lights went out. Could you please check my car for me? I left it parked in my driveway. Maybe in the morning you could see if it still has a problem."

The next day after checking the car, my brother came to see me. He said, "How did you drive home?" I said, "What do you mean?" He said, "Your alternator is out. It is not working at all." Archie let me know that without the alternator working, the car can do nothing. I knew then for sure that yes, God did take care of us and got us home, even with no alternator working. I knew He heard my dashboard prayer.

Another time I had a close call in my car. After going over a railroad track the car just stopped. I safely coasted into a parking lot. A mechanic came and looked at it. He let me know that it was a good thing the car stopped when it did because whatever steered that car was broken and, because it stopped, we were safe.

I learned a while back to always pray for my safety and the safety of anyone else who was in my car with me. I was glad that I learned years ago to ask God to protect me and my passengers in my car. He listened to my prayer and let me see a couple of the miracles He was always ready to work. I am sure He worked many others I didn't even know about.

"Rejoice always, pray without ceasing, in everything give for this is the will of God in Christ Jesus for you." (1 Thessalonians 5:16-18)

Tender Mercies

—Dorothy Wiggins

L arry and I were married twelve years. We wanted so dearly to have a baby. We tried hard and prayed diligently for a child. Finally, the Lord saw fit and I was expecting a baby. The baby was born by cesarean because I was bleeding to death. I was dying and so was my baby. God pulled me through. My little baby lived for a short two hours.

I figured we were married twelve years and I'm a child of God. I got the Holy Ghost when I was six years old. I started saying to God, "God, I don't understand this. I mean, I lived for You all my life." I even started blaming my loving husband saying, "Larry, what did you do wrong?" There's got to be some reason why this happened. He said, "Honey, there is nothing wrong that we have done. We are human and this is a God thing. We have to put it in His Hands."

It was so difficult for me. I never got to even hold my baby. I was so ill and the doctor, knowing me, came in and sat down by me. I wanted to see my baby. He said, "Dorothy, I just believe the best thing for you is not to do that. I think if you ever hold him you will bond and it would be better that you don't."

You know what? I believe when I get to Heaven, I am going to bond when I see my baby. I don't know if he'll be a little baby or if he's going to be a twenty-one-year-old young man. I'm going to wrap my arms around him and tell him all those months I carried him I loved him so much and I am so happy that finally I get to hold him in my arms.

When he was born I heard that little weak cry and many nights later I would wake still hearing that little sound. If it wouldn't be for my husband I wouldn't have made it. He would comfort me and pray for me and the arms of God would come in and lift me. God never let me go.

It took me a long time to accept this. In the beginning I was so bitter and I couldn't understand. I still don't understand, but that's okay. God just works out things so beautifully. The very next year our son Forrest was born and he is the baby God wanted us to have, so he became our baby. God blessed us with our son Forrest and he has been the joy and pride of our life. God does all things well.

"And I give them eternal life, and they shall never perish; neither shall anyone snatch them out of My hand." (John 10:28)

Crossing Many Waters

– Ellinor Nieto

I was twenty-one years old when I decided to go to America. I had a friend in New Rochelle, New York. She sent me the information I needed to go to the USA. I went to the American Consulate to speak with the Consul who was a lady. After she completed my paperwork she asked, "Why do you want to go to America?" I said to her, "You are American, aren't you?" She said,

"Yes! But, if you stay here a while longer, I will offer you a job at my house. I have four little boys and when my position here in London is complete, we will all move to Washington, DC. You can come with us if you decide to take the position. I really need a nanny for my four boys and I would love for you to be the nanny."

She told me I could stay with her and the family until it was time to leave and it would be so good. She would be helping me and I would be helping her. She was so down to earth and such a very nice lady. I was sorry I could not take her up on her offer. I explained that I had to be true to the party who had sponsored me to go to America. She understood and told me if anything happened and my plans didn't turn out right, to call her. She gave me her card and let me know she really wanted and needed me. She would be there if ever I needed her.

After the Consulate helped me acquire all the papers for my journey, I went to the shipping office. I asked the shipping clerk for a ship that didn't rock because I get sea-sick. He said that the Queen would never rock and I would never get sea-sick on her. He said, "The Queen Mary! That is the one I will put you on. I promise you that you will not get sea-sick on her. No one gets sea-sick on the Queen Mary!"

When I was on that Queen Mary I wish I would have had that guy next to me. I was so sea-sick for so many days I wanted to die. If that guy would have been there I would have choked him. That is what I wanted to do. That Queen Mary rocked up and down, and under and over and I kept thinking of that guy who got me on this ship, his famous Queen Mary. It was November 23, 1955, a most awful day and I wanted to choke that guy every second. I will never forget that day and the three days after. For those long four days I was deathly ill from that sea.

A nurse came to my cabin and gave me a green apple. It was as green as my face and it was so sour.

I thought it would make me sicker than I was already. I listened to the nurse and ate some. That apple did help. But that was not an enjoyable trip for sure. I kept thinking it was a good thing that the shipping agent was still in his office in London because his trip wouldn't have been enjoyable either.

"The voice of the Lord is over the waters; The God of glory thunders; The Lord is over many waters."
(Psalm 29:3)

Loretha with those beautiful curls

God Takes Care of Us

—Loretha Ward

I t all started on November 27, 1936 when Allen Doyle married Lois Willis one night during his revival in Gladewater, Texas by Rev. E.T. Gary. Afterwards, they went right on with service that night and people received the Holy Ghost. One year later on November 19, 1937, I was born. My dad continued his work of preaching the gospel as he had for several years.

During my childhood, I was able to witness the anointing of God and many miracles. Some stand out to me more than others. Some I saw with my own eyes. Others I remember because my parents told me of them. One I especially remember was concerning me. When I was about a year old I had a serious case of impetigo. Literally, I was covered with sores from head to toe. My granddaddy Willis took me to the doctor and the doctor said he could give me something, but it would take a year to cure me and I would be scarred for life.

Mother and Daddy took me to a fellowship meeting in Kilgore, Texas that night. They prayed and I was completely healed in three days. Today I don't have a single scar from that disease. God is good. During my childhood, God was our Healer. Mom and Dad didn't use a doctor and God always came to our rescue healing us many times.

God supplied for our needs in numerous ways during my lifetime. There was no money often while I was growing up. We lived in the back of the church and we were "keeping evangelists." One day Mother said, "If I just had an egg I'd bake a cake." A little while later we heard a noise in the church and Daddy went to see what it was. Somehow a chicken had gotten in the church and laid an egg. All the windows were closed and no one ever figured out how it got there. Is this hard to believe? I learned God was and is interested in the small things as well as the big ones.

We moved to Diboll, Texas. It was there at the age of nine that I received the Baptism of the Holy Ghost and His gift of speaking in tongues. I was baptized in the Name of Jesus in a pond on one of the member's property. I remember Mother had curled my hair and she wanted me to wait, but no, I had to go ahead and be baptized.

I have memories of going with Daddy when he preached in other places and I would play the piano and sing. I also went with Wilma Nix and played and sang for her revival in Dayton, Texas. All the time, I believe God was preparing me for the work He wanted me to do.

"Therefore humble yourselves under the mighty hand of God, that He may exalt you in due time, casting all your care upon Him, for He cares for you." (1 Peter 5:6-7)

His Name Was Michael

—Bertha Brooks Johnson

O ne Friday afternoon, after I had picked up my pay check, my youngest daughter Kathy and I left the house to get my other daughter Jackie. She was still at school practicing track with her team. The thought came to me, "Bertha, don't cash your check yet." But, I thought, "Oh, but I want to." So I went on and cashed it. I realized also that my car was low on gas and it would be wise to stop and fill my car at that time. I just went ahead though thinking, "No. I can make it." I didn't want to stop. I chose not to obey the thought God had given me.

So, I drove all the way out to Jackie's high school and picked her up. We were in the car driving back home on Hardy Road. After a distance on that road, my car ran out of gas. Hardy Road only had two lanes, one going one way, one going the other. We had stopped in a very deserted place.

I pulled off to the side onto a small patch of grass. I didn't have a cell phone in those days. There was no place where I could go knock on a door and ask somebody for help. It was getting dark and I worried for the safety of my daughters and myself.

On my left side, there was traffic going in the opposite direction. Cars coming up behind me had to pass my car carefully. On the right side where I had to pull over were railroad tracks. I realized I should have not wasted time cashing my check and should have used my time wisely to stop and get gas. I asked the Lord to forgive me for not listening to what He had put into my mind to do. He had clearly told me I did not need to cash that check and I needed gas in my car. I didn't obey His urgings.

Some young boys kept driving past us, giggling and laughing as they did. They were playing their music very loud in their car as they continued to go back and forth passing my car. I had a bad feeling and my instincts told me that they might be planning to do harm to my girls and me.

I began to pray and ask God to forgive me and I began to forgive myself. A peace came over me. I looked in my rearview mirror, I saw a man who was driving an old fashion red, white and silver truck. He got out of the truck and came to me and said, "You know it is dangerous what you did." I said, "Yes sir. I know it is." He said, "Stay in your car and I am going to get you some gas." Then, he left.

He took off so quickly. I had a hard time watching him as he left. I knew there was no gas station near. Yet, he returned so quickly. He was behind me again before I even noticed his truck returning. He came to my side and told me to stay in the car again, reminding me of the danger. He noticed those boys passing as he put the gas into my car.

I got out of the car and asked him if he wanted any payment for the gas. He said, "No." I asked, "What is your name?" He said very sternly in a way I've never heard anyone speak before, "Michael!" The sternness was not from anger. It sounded to me like he spoke with a voice full of power. I will never forget the way he said his name.

Once he put the gas in my car and made sure my car started and we were safe and ready to go, he drove off in front of me. I thought of following him, but his truck went on ahead very quietly and quickly, disappearing in a very short time. I will always remember that man. I do believe he was an angel sent by God. His name was Michael. I call him my Michael because God sent him to me when my daughters and I needed to be protected. When I got home, I thanked the Lord for taking care of us that day and I promised to be more obedient to His urgings.

"The Lord is near to those who have a broken heart, And saves such as have a contrite spirit."
(Psalm 34:18)

Gift of Sight

– Dwight E.

God worked a miracle in my life a long time ago and I still remember it. I was born blind. When I was about two years old, my mom brought me to church. She was praying for me. I heard her praying. God healed me and I could see and my eyes are still great. I can even read very small print and I don't need glasses.

We were a huge family. I grew up with ten brothers and sisters. I was the second from the bottom. We were poor, honest and hardworking. I grew up in a home that didn't have a lot of money. We didn't have much education. We had faith and God gave us miracles. I am one.

When I was seven years old a nice man who became my friend taught me his trade. He was a Jew and had been in a German concentration camp for years. I even saw the numbers that were written on his arm. He would always be working so hard in his shop repairing boots and shoes. He was glad for the work he did.

One day I was passing by his shop and he said, "Come on in

here and I will teach you a trade."
I was very young and when I heard
him say, "I'll help you make money
for the rest of your life," it sounded
good to me.

I listened and worked and worked
and listened. That man who taught
me was a master teacher. He taught
me how to learn, made me want to
learn and to keep on learning. He
didn't let me give up. It took months
to learn just to put heels on those
shoes. Then, I learned to actually
put soles on the shoes, too.

I almost forgot my master teacher's promise that I would make lots
of money. I worked every day and
then one day I realized how hard I
was working and how much money

I wasn't earning. I mentioned this to my master teacher and told him maybe I should start my own business. I think he got worried, because he finally started paying me a little.

I began saving as much money as I could. I was still only making fifteen dollars a week. For years I didn't get a raise. My teacher was making very much money and he wasn't that willing to share with me for my hard work. I began to think out loud, "You know what? You have taught me to fix shoes for myself. I really appreciate what you have taught me and I think it would be well to seriously open my own shop." He was surprised and said,

"My goodness! I need to give you a raise." He didn't want to lose me.

He kept on paying me those fifteen dollars a week. He forgot the raise, but I kept working with him and saving. I would not have found a master teacher like him anywhere else. When he died I had saved enough to finally start my own business. I found a machine that I needed to repair shoes for $5000 and had enough. I bought everything I needed and soon my own shop was ready for customers.

I looked around at my shop and said, "Goodness gracious! Look at this!" I liked what I saw. I had my own business. It felt so good; I liked my job. I started working in my own shop and before I knew it I had piles and piles of shoes and boots to work on. I slept in the back of the shop and would find so many shoes every morning left in the front for me to fix. It was something so wonderful.

I worked hard every day, all day. Before I knew it, I had so much money, I could retire. It was such a great trade that my friend taught me. I am so grateful for these memories. They make me smile.

"The laborer is worthy of his wages." (1 Timothy 5:18)

Harry smiles listening to his sweet Joyce's music.

Someday

—Joyce Wiggins

My darling husband Harry Wiggins passed away December 30, 2011. I sent this message to him in heaven:

After you were gone my sweet love, I realized how closely our lives were tied together. You were always in my thoughts and in every decision I made. The last words you said to me were, "Thank you for taking care of me." I told you something like, "It is my pleasure. There is no place in the world I would rather be than by your side."

I was asking God for at least six more years with you, at least until you would be ninety. But, God wanted you sooner. You've been a wonderful, faithful husband for sixty-three years and a wonderful father to our three daughters, Linda, Beverly and Karen. You were the only boy I ever dated.

We were always able to discuss anything that came our way in a calm respectful way. We prayed together each day. We apologized often. I hope you've been as happy as I have been these sixty-three years. I will see you again soon my darling. Be waiting at the pearly gates for me.

I had hoped that we would go up in the rapture together but I will be here with our children, grand-children and great-grand-children you have adored and prayed for. Good-bye my darling for now. I miss you so much and love you with all my heart. I know you now have no pain and are with Jesus and with all our family and friends who have gone home, too.

Someday, someday soon my darling we will meet again.

"Blessed are the pure of heart for they shall see God." (Matthew 5:8)

Ready in a Quiet Place

– Berta Hinojosa

January 31, 2013, I had an appointment with my neurologist. I really didn't feel well. I was out of breath. My whole body began to feel useless and so weak. That is part of how my system is since I have Myasphenia Gravis. By the time the doctor saw me, my right eye was half closed, my left eye began to close and I had double vision. I couldn't do a thing about it. I became really out of breath. The doctor told me I was to go to the hospital immediately. I told him I was fine. He said, "Your heart is about to stop. You need to go to the emergency room right away."

I went home. My husband helped me get things ready. Then, he took me to the hospital. By the time we got the admission papers, I felt so much at peace. I felt like I was literally floating in a very beautiful place. I hadn't taken any medicine and I know hospitals are not beautiful. That feeling of peace and beauty was a gift from God to me and I knew it.

I was put in ICU right away and the doctors came in and explained to my husband what was going on. I told my husband if this is the way I am to go, it is a beautiful way. I told him, "I feel like I am in a peaceful garden holding hands with Jesus. I am not scared." I started singing the song, "In the Garden." My husband said, "No. You're not dying." I said, "If I am, it is okay. It is so peaceful."

Doctors soon came in and hooked me up to medication and I just continued to rest in that peace. I was in ICU for four days until I became stable. I was moved to a regular room and put on the medication Mestinon. I was kept in isolation and could have no visitors. I could and did have a couple of phone calls. Everyone made sure that I would not have any stress or anxiety during this time so the medicine would do what it was supposed to.

While I was in the hospital, I did a lot of thinking and was making plans. A doctor asked me if I had accepted my condition and told me it would be "touch and go" from now on. Well, I have accepted it. Really I have embraced it. It will be hard for my husband and my daughters but I have accepted what God has planned for me. I hope that they with all their hearts will do the same. I have told the doctors and my family when God wants me to be with Him forever, I do not want to be resuscitated. I don't want my life to be prolonged. I have made my peace with God. I know the way I have felt; what I have gone through...love, hope, peace and pain. In faith, I know I am going to a better place. I love my family and look forward to holding each of them close to my heart when God finally says to me, "Come, Berta. Let Me take you Home."

"For as the heavens are high above the earth, So great is His mercy toward those who fear Him." (Psalm 103:11)

Nanny in Sweden

– Ellinor Nieto

W hen I was a teenager I was in school taking classes in home economics. After two years I completed the course in flying colors. I got top grade in my classes. I still have a picture of that black and white suit I made for the final grade. That type of suit was called *"pepita,"* and was very intricate. After the classes had been completed the overseer told me of a friend who was looking for a nanny for her two children.

I agreed to go for the position. I had to leave my home in Germany to take that job in far-away Sweden. It was a great opportunity. I thought, "click, click, click" and knew this was what I should do. I said, "Am I interested? I am ready to go tomorrow." My overseer got in contact with the family, arranged transportation and I was on my way.

I left on a train. It took about a day for me to get to my new home in Sweden. The lady of the house met me at the train station. She took me to the house and gave me a lovely room that was to be my own. The next morning I met the children, five-year-old Carrie and two-year-old Lena.

Carrie was a lot like me, stubborn, when we first met. I got the best of her and in the end she wouldn't leave my side. We would walk to the park with Lena in the carriage and Carrie holding my hand as tightly as she could. We lived in a very large beautiful apartment in the winter. During the summer we stayed in a little cottage in a small fishing village. Everyone in the village wore wooden shoes. They had blue leather on top and wood on the bottom. We all wore these. Even little Lena had a tiny pair.

There was a restaurant in the village where the three of us would go. The owner would see us coming and he would say, "Here are the little *"tisks."* That was his Swedish nickname for us. He would tease us because we always wanted the same thing on his menu, white potatoes with meat and eggs. It was really delicious. He always knew what we wanted without even asking.

There was a beautiful church in that fishing village, right by the sea. It stood all by itself surrounded by sand. I would tell the children, "Take off your shoes. We are going into a holy place." *"Clocs"* are the Swedish word for shoes. As soon as I would say, "Let's take off our *clocs*," they did and I did, too. We were going to walk on holy ground. Our shoes stayed outside. Those little ones got used to it and sometimes a half a mile away from the church, they would want to take off their *"clocs,"* but they waited until I took off mine. They were so little, but they learned so quickly.

I had a good time being the nanny for these little girls. Their mother worked in Copenhagen making hats. She worked at this specialty every day. So, I was in charge of the household. I had the money, purchased what was needed and cared for the children and the house.

The husband had polio in his left hand. His wife wanted me to massage his hand because that was a treatment he needed. I felt strange about doing that but I did it, rubbing it with mineral oil. I massaged it every day for weeks. Finally, one day, he could use his hand well enough to ride his own bicycle. All of us would ride bikes around the village. Lena rode in a special seat on my bike. Little Carrie rode her bike and it added to their enjoyment when their father could ride along on their trips.

Their mother was hard working and very kind. She would come home every day after a long day at work and still wash the clothes. I hung them upstairs and ironed them when they were dry. I enjoyed all the work assigned me. It was never too hard. When the mother came home from work, she always did as much as she could and she always appreciated what I did. Once she created something special for me at her place of work. It was a hat she made to match my light gray mohair coat. She even made that hat of light gray mohair. I still have a picture of that beautiful hat made just for me.

While I was working in the home as a nanny for these little girls I loved to draw pictures for them. Their mother saw my drawings and said I was very talented. She registered me in an art school and sent me to painting classes there every Tuesday from 7:00 p.m. until 9:00 p.m. Her mother, who owned the best chocolate factory in the city, came and baby-sat for the children.

She would bring all kinds of chocolates for the children and for me. I would find my treats when I would return home from my classes. I had a good time there and those were the best chocolates I ever ate.

In that art school in 1955, I completed two beautiful oil paintings. The first painting was a "Christmas Flower," the second is a still life painting. The glass in that picture looked real enough to touch. I started a painting of a little child. I really enjoyed doing that painting, too. I didn't complete that one because my walking shoes started "itching." I needed to move on.

It was very difficult to leave this home I had grown to love. I was offered another position as nanny in England and had signed the contract. I thought everything was going to be fine. I went back to Germany all decked out in my beautiful hat and coat and before I had even settled back in my home, there was an emergency phone call for me. The two little girls were inconsolable. Their mother was on the phone saying they did not even want to eat. They were crying day and night for me to come back.

My heart was breaking. I wanted to turn around and go back. I talked to both of my little friends and told them other children needed a nanny more now and I had to go and take care of other children. They understood. Then Carrie had an idea. She said to her daddy, "Papi, you need to adopt our nanny, so she can be our big sister forever." And little Lena started shouting, "Yes, yes, yes!" It definitely wasn't easy leaving this family.

This first job was a parting with many tears, but I had to be true to my contract I almost gave up and turned back. I knew how much those little girls would miss me and I them. Even on the boat when I was leaving, I was crying. I was still crying in the train at night. I even asked the conductor if there was a train going back. I was tempted to return and surprise them. But, I went on because I knew I had to be true to God's plan for me. It also was God's plan for that family because my leaving caused the mother and father to spend more time together with each other and their girls. I learned later that instead of getting me for a big sister they got a new baby brother.

"In Him we have obtained an inheritance, being predestined according to the purpose of Him who works all things according to the counsel of His will..." (Ephesians 1:11)

Mr. Laxton gets the big one.

My Daddy, the Fisherman

— Sanny Laxton

The earliest memories I have are of going floundering with my family. I was small because my mother was holding me and I was watching the lanterns move back and forth. My dad, my uncle and my grandpa would have long spear like poles and we'd all go down to the beach in Galveston.

They would walk back and forth in the shallow water and when they would feel that flounder under their feet or see it, they would spear it. I remember that dad would tell me how the flounder would come and bury themselves under the sand.

When I would walk in the water, my daddy would tell me to be very careful where I walked because stingrays bury themselves under the sand just like the flounders and they would really hurt me if I stepped on them. I learned to walk and wade very carefully in that shallow water. With care I learned to see their outline in the sand.

When Daddy wasn't fishing or floundering, he would go "oyster hunting." He would come back with sacks of oysters from his trips. I learned to shuck those oysters in no time. I could open them very fast and eat them just as quickly.

There was a large tree that my mom would stand under with me while the men would go fishing, catch flounders, or go "oyster hunting." One day many years later I was driving past that spot where my family would go on those outings and I recognized that tree. I was reminded of our fishing trips those many years ago.

"Then Jesus said to them, 'Follow Me, and I will make you become fishers of men.' They immediately left their nets and followed Him."
(Mark 1:17-18)

A Song When I Needed It

– Dorothy Wiggins

I n my story today, with the Lord's help, I want to lift you up, inspire you, and let you know the Lord cares. Several years ago, my choir director asked me to learn a song to sing in our choir. He said, "You're singing a solo and the choir will back you up." I said, "Okay. I'll try." He gave me a tape so I could learn the song. I got home, popped the tape into the tape recorder and I began to listen.

I started crying. When I practiced, I would cry so hard, I couldn't sing. I tried it for several days and each time I'd hear the words, I would start bawling.

I called my choir director and told him, "You have to get someone else. I just can't do this because I'll just get up there and cry. He said, "Then, you'll just have to cry. You're going to do it." So, I guess by the time I got up there to sing, I had cried it all out. What happened was…I needed that song and its words were blessing me so much.

I got to talk with the lady who wrote the song, Wanda Weeks Phillips. She shared that she had written that song, "Underneath Are His

Everlasting Arms," when her mother had just passed away, a very sad time in her life. She said she was standing at her kitchen sink feeling like she just could not go on; that her load was too heavy. She said, "I was saying Lord, I can't carry this. I can't go on." All at once, she said, she felt His arms under her pulling her close. Immediately the Scripture came to her mind, "Underneath are His everlasting arms." At that point she went and began to write the words to the song I was asked to sing.

The reason that song touched me so much was at that time the song was given to me, I was taking care of my mother who had Alzheimer's. I was so stressed at the time. This song was giving me such peace, to just know that underneath it all were the Lord's everlasting arms. That song had been given to me at the time I needed it most.

"The eternal God is your refuge, And underneath are the everlasting arms." (Deuteronomy 33:27)

Dreams Bring Healing

—Paulette Meeks

I want to share with you about a special time when God gave me my most personal miracle that lasted about a week and a half. It all began as I was praying one night for some friends I had visited in a near-by nursing home. I was struck profoundly by the loneliness I felt some of my friends were living through. Their sadness was great since they felt alone in their many losses.

As I prayed, God let me realize that He would take care of them and He would take care of me, too. I went to sleep experiencing a quiet and lasting peace. And I dreamed. When I awakened the next morning, I remembered the entire dream. It was so clear, not confusing as dreams usually are, at least, to me.

I immediately felt blessed and went to my computer to write the memory of that dream. I didn't know why I wanted to record it. I just knew I should. I placed it in my documents on my computer and labeled it "my dreams." I knew this was just the beginning.

The next night I went to bed and the dream continued. When I awoke,

I knew God had blessed me again as He had the night before. I went to my computer and recorded the second night of dreams. The dreams continued for about eleven nights. Every night I could hardly wait to go to sleep. It was like going to a movie, a movie about so many blessings God had given me during my life.

In the morning when I would sit at my computer, I didn't even have to think. The memory of each dream would just come alive and recording it was as if God was pouring such awareness of His loving care into my heart all the way through my fingertips. I realized He was helping me really know of His Presence throughout my life.

When the last dream was given to me, the Lord let me realize how much a treasure He had truly shared with me by giving me my husband, my dearest friend. It was a hard dream to stay with because I re-lived saying, "Good-bye" to my love again, giving him my permission to leave me. Jesus was calling him Home. He certainly didn't need my permission, but God wanted me to give it and I did again in my dream. But, here I saw my sweetheart so well, so free in the loving embrace of our Father and how happy this love of my life was. I remembered especially his last smile to me and I realized that our bond so cemented in God Himself, was stronger than ever. And now, this wondrous God honored that gift by blessing me with this miracle of dreams in the night.

"Your sons and your daughters shall prophesy. Your young men shall see visions. Your old men shall dream dreams. And on My menservants and on My maidservants I will pour out My Spirit in those days." (Acts 2:17-18)

Baby Sarah

Angels Keep Watch

– Sarah Duplease

When I was a little baby we lived in a simple house way out in the country. We didn't have locks on doors and there were not many other houses around us. One day my mother was in the back yard washing clothes in a tub. I had one brother and three sisters who were probably in school at the time. I was crawling around I guess just doing what a baby does, going wherever I could.

Apparently I had wandered off without her knowing it. My mom told me this story many times. While she was doing that washing, she heard a voice saying, "Where is Sarah?"

She went looking for me right away. She looked all over. I wasn't in the house. She had no idea where I had gone.

Finally she decided to look outside. I wasn't in the yard close to the house. I had wandered down the driveway and fell into the ditch. She found me and said I was in water holding on to blades of grass. I was so fortunate that she heard that angel and went to find me. I know God took care of me and I wouldn't be here today if He hadn't sent His angel to my mother that day I crawled off.

Another time God was looking out for me was when I was a toddler. I kept Him busy. I was wandering around again, this time walking. I headed for the street and no one in my family knew I was on my way. I was already on the pavement of that street.

My dad was working in the yard repairing the motor of a truck, and this time he got the message that something was the matter. He knew he needed to look for me. As he approached the street a huge harvesting truck was coming and there I was in the street unaware of the danger. That truck was barreling down on me. My dad went running across the street and picked me up just in time. My life was saved again. When I think about this I am touched again by the love God has for me. I know He saved me at these times. I wonder how many other times He sent angels to protect me from dangers.

"Behold, I send an Angel before you to keep you in the way and to bring you into the place which I have prepared. (Exodus 23:20)

Cookie Answers

—Ellinor Nieto

When I was very young, about four years old, I had a nickname "Cookie" which was a special name of love given me by my mother and grandparents. The circus came to town and I was all excited. My grandpa took me and we were sitting right in front. I could see everything. The clowns came out and were so funny.

One very tall clown was standing right near me. There was another little short clown not far from him. The tall clown kept saying, "Cookie, where are you?" I looked at my grandpa and said, "He's calling me." My grandpa was looking at other performers and I think he didn't know what I was saying. He said to me, "Yes, you go if he is calling you. Just go to him."

The clown called again, "Cookie, Cookie, where are you?" So, I said as loudly as I could, "I'm here." I stood up and said it again, "I'm here." Then I walked up to him. He said, "Are you Cookie?" I said, "Yes, I'm Cookie." "Oh, okay, Cookie," he said to the short clown. "You don't

have to come. I've got Cookie here."
Everybody clapped. My grandpa
had his eye on me, watching me
and I wasn't afraid of those clowns
because that big one knew my name.

*"For God has not given us a
spirit of fear, but of power and
of love and of a sound mind."*
(Timothy 1:7)

A Simple Purchase, a Lasting Gift

−Dave Kasprzak

June of 1982, I was in the retail auto parts business. I sold a little #1157 NA light bulb. That is an amber colored light bulb for a turn signal on many cars built in the 60's, 70's, and 80's. I didn't know it, but this woman came into the store and spent about half of her paycheck the month earlier buying parts for an old junk Camaro she had.

She came in again, trying to meet me. She saw me and the Lord had blessed her with me not seeing her. I was not someone to look at in those days and I definitely wasn't looking for anyone. I was going through a really rough time in my life and I had just told one of my co-workers, "If I ever get seriously involved with another woman, just shoot me."

God had other plans. That day... the woman and I met. She bought her "light *bub*" as she called it and walked out of the auto parts store. When she walked out that door, I turned around and looked at the co-worker I had talked to earlier and said, "Did you see the eyes on that woman?" He looked at me and I continued, "I take back what I said earlier. I think I just met the woman I am going to marry."

I found out later on that when she left, she went directly to her best friend's house screaming at the top of her lungs. Her friend's daddy came running to the door thinking somebody was shot or killed. We went out and seriously began dating. In about one and a half years later, on December 3, 1983, we married. I can say I am a much better man today because of this woman who came into my life that day so many years ago.

The Lord has been with both of us through thick and thin. There have been major illnesses, tragedies and

God has been with us through it all. The other day I read an article about the stages of marriage. It went something like this: In the beginning when there are no children, most couples are extremely happy. Kids come and the happiness diminishes a bit. The time period that seems to bring the most unhappiness is when the kids are teenagers. I just know it seems to take a very long time to get from thirteen years old to twenty-five.

I've heard that the happiest time for a man and wife is the "empty nest" years. That is what the article stated, too. Rosemary and I were talking about that and we both agree it is that way for us. Our love story continues each day better and better in our empty nest. I am so glad that little lady came to purchase a simple light bulb many years ago. The Lord had His own purchase in mind for the both of us and I am so grateful His plans are so much greater than our own.

"We know all things work together for those who love God, to those who are the called according to His purpose." (Romans 8:28)

Young Pastors Jerry and Loretha Ward

Preacher's Kid and More

—Loretha Ward

W hen I was very young, my daddy pastored in Jacksonville, Texas. There was a family there by the name of Ward. They had six children and one was a boy named Jerry Don Ward. We played together and he said one day that I pushed him into a tub of water. He just didn't know about that "preacher's kid." That's what he called me. We moved away from Jacksonville when I was about six years old.

I met Jerry again as a teenager. It was at a Youth Conference in Lufkin, Texas. He had grown into a very handsome young man. He remembered the "preacher's kid" and our friendship was rekindled. Soon he was standing on my front doorstep. On October 13, 1956, I became Mrs. Jerry Ward. My husband soon felt the call to preach.

I thought he would start out a "seasoned preacher" like my dad. Well, his first sermons lasted ten to fifteen minutes. I remember him being pleased as he spoke with a former pastor. He said, "Brother Stevens, I preached for seventeen minutes last night." I think that was for Brother Forrest Ford in Houston, Texas.

After a few sermons, he started preaching full time. He met the Texas Board for license and told them about it. One minister said, "You really must have lots of faith."

Jerry said, "Yes sir. I know it." Those short sermons didn't continue. Before long, it was hard to keep him to just one hour. God anointed him with an evangelistic ministry and he could not be stopped. Bringing God's message took us across the country. There is no miracle greater than watching souls being born into the Kingdom of God. In evangelistic work we both witnessed hundreds.

In teaching God's Word, we saw people start as Christians. In pastoring we were able to help them grow and develop into mature Christians. God blessed us with four pastorates during our ministry: Seabrook, Silsbee, Paris and Houston. We were able to participate in the lives of so many of

God's children by teaching them in home and church the Word of God, encouraging, praying with them, marrying the young and burying the old.

There's not space to tell of all the miracles we witnessed during our ministry. I'll only mention one that happened in Silsbee, Texas. A couple brought their little five-year-old boy who couldn't walk to Sunday morning service for prayer. We took a lot of time praying for him that morning and he left not being able to walk. That afternoon while playing, he got up and walked. He's walked ever since. Because of that miracle, his mother, dad, uncle and cousins came to church, were baptized and received the Holy Ghost.

His uncle had never been to church and was known in that town as a very rough fighter. He was totally against the church. After he was saved, he couldn't do enough to support his *former opponent.* The town took notice and others came and joined our church because of him and the miracle God worked in his life.

Jerry and I were blessed witnessing to many people: alcoholics, drug addicts, the hurting, the sick, rich, poor, lawyers, doctors, educated, homeless and anyone searching for God. We witnessed their lives change drastically. The first thing they all wanted was to praise God for His miracles in the lives of their families and friends.

What a privilege to give one's life to the Kingdom of God. In my old age I love to meet up with those who became a part of our ministry. I cherish all the memories of what God has done. As the song says, "There's something better than gold" and another, "I've never regretted one mile I've traveled for the Lord."

"...that you may know ...the hope of His calling...the exceeding greatness of His power toward us who believe..." (Ephesians 1:19-20)

Storm Shopping

—Sanny Laxton

My first long trip with my family was a trip to New Orleans. I was probably around four years old. We were going there to see the city and to go shopping. My mother had decided we would leave home on a Friday night. So, we packed up and my dad started that long drive. It began raining and the wind was blowing hard.

We crossed over the bridge and entered Louisiana. My daddy laughed and stopped the car for all of us to see. He said, "Look at those big crawfish!" There on the road in front of us were these crawfish with their claws up like telling us to "Stop!" It was so funny. They looked like traffic police trying to stop us. They would just stand up and wave their claws at us.

We got into New Orleans around six or seven o'clock in the morning. There were tree branches in the road and some roads were closed because of all the debris thrown all over. We stopped at a grocery store and went in. My brother and I were so excited because they had those double coned ice-creams and we wanted one. We had never seen them before.

While we were enjoying our treat, the guy in the store told my daddy that those branches were all over the road because a hurricane had just passed through that area last night. So, we had driven right through that hurricane and didn't even know it. God took care of us in the midst of that storm and didn't even let us know it was all around us.

We drove along the river and crossed over the bridge to Metairie. There was a place there with slot machines and my brother and I got to play them. We didn't get to see much more of New Orleans though, since there was so much storm damage. So, we just went back on Highway 90 and returned home.

We knew what it was like to live through hurricanes. Once, one hit our home town. Our house shook so much. We thought it would fall apart. It didn't, but the best part was the outhouse. We had a lot of pine oak trees all around our yard. They were very tall and strong. One hurricane came through and blew them all down. The only thing standing where the trees were was our outhouse which was right in the middle. It was stronger than those trees. We thought that was funny.

Later, when I was older I was invited to go shopping in Houston. We went to North Shore to shop first. My daughter wanted something in one of the stores there. While we were in the store, we heard a loud sound. Immediately, almost everyone ran out of the building. I just moved up in the line to check out. The people came back and they started talking about what had happened. It was an explosion. A ship in the channel had exploded and it was so great it actually shook the store we were in.

After this experience, we went on to the Wal-Mart in Houston. We shopped for quite a while. When we came out, the parking lot was filled with water. I had to wade in knee-deep water to get to the truck. When we got back home I asked what happened. We found out that while we were in that Wal-Mart a hurricane had hit that area.

Another time my mother wanted me to take her shopping in Beaumont. We drove there and when we got into the store, the sales lady asked why we were out. She told us a hurricane was headed our way. We left quickly and returned home. After that, when anyone would ask me to go shopping, I decided to check the weather news first. I figured I had enough shopping days with hurricanes either leading or following me.

"And suddenly a great tempest arose…His disciples came to Him…He rebuked the winds…

and there was a great calm."
(Matthew 8:24-26)

Am I Useful to God?

—Joyce Wiggins

One day I was just sitting in our snow cone stand that we operated. I was really not working and felt I was wasting time. Our stand was very close to the street. I didn't want to feel useless, so I started to pray. There was a lady who kept walking back and forth near the stand. She would walk in front of the stand, then turn and come back again. She did this twice.

I thought maybe she was trying to decide if she wanted a snow cone or not. Finally, she turned, walked up to the window and said, "I don't understand this at all but, when I was passing your stand something kept telling me to come up to this window and someone would help me." I said, "Ma'am, I don't know a lot of things, but I do know the Lord and He can solve every problem."

I then told the woman to go around to the side door and invited her in. She came in and began to tell me how broken hearted she was. Her daughter had run away. Her husband was pretty rough on the girl and she didn't know how to handle it.

I began to pray for her and told her God would give her peace in this situation. I prayed God would give her wisdom so she would know what she was to do. I prayed for each member of her family. After I prayed a while and looked at her, she seemed a different person. Calmness had come over her.

She breathed a big sigh of relief and said, "Oh, I feel so good." She smiled. Jesus had touched her because she turned to Him and trusted Him. She hugged me before she left and told me she was going down to a nearby park to find a quiet place to pray.

Jesus proved to me that day in my snow cone stand, no matter where we are, no matter what we're doing or not doing, we can always be useful to Him if we have the desire to reach out to Him.

"Silver and gold I do not have, but what I do have I give you; in the name of Jesus Christ..." (Acts 3:6)

Beth ready for square dancing

Memories Come Full Circle

– Beth Davidson

School was always fun for me. In high school, I enjoyed many extra-curricular activities. I played the saxophone in the school concert band and marching band. I also sang in the choir in middle school. In high school I loved to roller skate and square dance. My square dance team took top honors at the Pennsylvania State Farm Show and we even danced on TV at the KDKA television station. We were just family and friends who had grown up together and enjoyed dancing whenever we had the opportunity. We would go to the square dance caller's home, move all the furniture out of the way and then we'd dance until we could dance no more. Dancing was so much fun.

Church on Sunday was expected, but it was never a chore. We were taught early on about God. My parents were active in church and as we got older, we were also. Church camp in the summer was a highlight. Later, when I was in high school, I was a counselor at one of the camps. That was an enjoyable experience I remember to this day.

My older brother joined the Army. When he would come home on leave, one of his buddies would ride to his home with him. Brother wanted me to be a blind date for his Army buddy. I agreed and little did I know it would be the beginning of a romance that would last forever.

Thanks to that blind date, my sweet Bill and I found each other.

We have been married forty-six years and have two wonderful children and five treasured grand-children. When our children were young we watched them play basketball and baseball through the years. Now we enjoy the excitement all over again as we see our grand-children swim, be cheerleaders and play basketball, baseball and volleyball.

Our parents watched us grow much as we have watched our children through the years. My husband and I have come full circle now as we realize the need to care for our parents. Bill's mom and mine are widows and need our love and support just as we needed theirs through the years. They were there for us. Now, we do our best to be there for them.

My mom is ninety-one years old and too weak to live on her own. My sister Cynthia searched for the best care for her when it was needed and found it in an assisted living home. The transition was difficult but we knew it was the loving move to make. Mom is very happy and safe in her new home. She is getting the best care and attention and loves it. She has made friends, gets to go out with the group for lunch and the residence always has something going on that is fun and interesting for her.

My mother-in-law lives with Bill and me. We take care of her medical needs and doctor appointments when necessary. At eighty-four years of age, she is active with her reading, crocheting and using her computer. She can take care of herself but we don't want her living alone.

Now that my husband Bill and I are both retired, we have more opportunities to strengthen our family circle with love and support. We can work hard on our own projects without deadlines, care for each other with less rush, kick up our heels, sleep late, enjoy old memories, create new ones and each day grow closer together.

"Take heed…for one's life does not consist in the abundance of the things he possesses." (Luke 12:15)

Honeymoon

– Ellinor Nieto

Hector and I were back in New York. We got married on August 25, 1961. My friend was my bride's maid and Hector's friend was our best man. We packed our clothes and got ready to leave for our honeymoon in Bermuda. We arrived at Kennedy Airport and had a lovely luncheon. Then, we went over to the National Airlines counter and tried to get tickets for a flight down to Bermuda. We were told everything was sold out. We could try LaGuardia Airport and maybe we would find a spot there for us. They said they had a flight there, but it didn't look good seat wise.

We went by taxi from Kennedy Airport to La Guardia and when we got there we were told the flight was definitely overbooked. They said, "There is no chance for you to get on board for this flight." They told us then to try Newark Airport in New Jersey. So, we took another taxi from La Guardia Airport in New York to Newark Airport in New Jersey.

We carried our luggage as we went from airport to airport because we couldn't get checked in on any flight since they were all overbooked. There were no seats available for us on flights going to Bermuda. Here at Newark again we were told by the agent, "There are no seats available on this flight."

I was trembling and sitting on a bench. I told Hector, "I am going back home. This is crazy. We are spending everything on taxis and we haven't even begun to leave for Bermuda yet." He said, "Just wait a little more." So, I was ready to go to sleep on the wooden benches in the airport.

The National Airline agent came over to us and said, "There may be a chance for you to get a flight out of Newark New Jersey to Bermuda.

There's a departure at 3:00 a.m." I said, "3:00 a.m.?" "Yes," he said. "We have to wait for fifty passengers to come in and you will be passengers fifty-one and fifty-two. I booked you already because the flight is half-empty." I was ready to cry because I was so overjoyed I didn't know what to do. The guy had already checked us in on his list and I was so happy.

The plane was ready for passengers and we were brought on first. Only Hector and I were sitting there. The rest of the fifty passengers entered the plane. They were all nuns, fifty of them. They were going to some kind of a meeting in Bermuda. Hector said to me, "Do you think I could order a drink with those fifty nuns watching me?" The stewardess overheard him and she said, "I'm going to bring a good stiff drink for both of you." Hector said, "Hallelujah!" And we were off for our honeymoon in Bermuda.

"Eye has not seen, nor ear heard,
nor have entered into the heart
of man the things which God has
prepared for those who love Him."
(1 Corinthians 2:9)

God's Plan for Me

—Joe Marcom

My recent experience with heart surgery left me completely helpless for some time. The doctor's orders were that I was not to push, pull, or lift anything over five pounds and I could not drive. There was very little that I could do and I found myself wondering how I had arrived at my present situation.

In mid-October, 2012, though I was seventy-eight, I thought of myself generally as a man in good health. My wife and I were retired. We had enough money to get by on and our kids were grown. I figured I had at least ten or fifteen good years left to enjoy this life.

I was surprised when I found myself, almost over-night with a severe shortage of breath and pains that I couldn't identify. My children prevailed upon me to go to the ER and get checked out. The next thing I remember the doctor standing over me, telling me I needed a quad by-pass surgery. I did not expect this at all. I needed time to decide if I wanted this and if my family backed this decision. My family stood by me through it all. Two of my children even returned from their mission trip to be with me.

After surgery and a quick recuperation, instead of returning home, my daughter brought me to her home as my family continued supporting me in my return to health. They saw my need and jumped in whole-heartedly. What a blessing they have been. All of my life, I have been a pretty much "do-it-yourself" person and this care by my family touched me immensely.

I believe when you want a job done, you do it by yourself if you are able. Even when I was recuperating from that major surgery, I had planned to do so by myself. God had other plans. My entire family was there for me. The sweet service they always gave me was not expected, but respected and appreciated.

While I was in the hospital, my wife became ill and needed emergency surgery. We both were in the hospital and our children were there supporting us in our needs. When it came time for us to go home, we both were given the most wonderful treatment in the homes of our children.

My wife Betty and I rescued small animals while we were well. After becoming ill, we were concerned about our small "friends" at home. To us, their welfare was as important as that of any other member of our family. Our children knew this and stepped in when we couldn't. Even one of our church members came to the rescue.

After a few days out of the hospital, I had a set-back and had to return for almost three weeks. This was pro-longed and my family and church family were constant and consistent in their love. They took care of personal needs and supported me by prayer and visits, making my convalescence a special journey. The doctor said today I am fine. God tells me He is not through with me yet.

It is difficult for me to imagine what makes me worth all of this. I do know with absolute certainty that God loves me just as I am. He has given me more in my family and in my church than I could ever pay back. He is always watching out for me personally. He is watching out for my family, too, and I would never want to stop any part of His plan. I am surrounded by His love and whatever comes along in the future, I am convinced I am beloved by God, as a man, a husband and a parent. While I enjoy the life God gives me now, I want to do anything and everything, through His power, to give Him glory every second.

"Humble yourselves…casting all your care upon Him, for He cares for you." (1 Peter 5:6-7)

Sanny and Judy ready to travel in that red MG

Vacation Changes

– Sanny Laxton

M y sister Judy and I were on our way to Colorado for a planned vacation. Our travels passed through Amarillo so we decided to call our cousin who was stationed there at the Air Force base. As we pulled into Amarillo, we stopped to call him. He told us to come on out to the Air Force base because our Uncle George had just died. He said we could stay in the barracks there and then we could after a night's rest, all go back to Houston for the funeral.

We arrived at the base and he brought us quietly into the barracks. We had to go upstairs so he went ahead of us saying, "Girls on the floor." He needed to warn the others so I guess Airmen wouldn't come out in underwear with us around.

The next morning, we were getting ready to leave. Judy and I had come in my little red MG sports car. It sat us both comfortably. He wanted to drive and he wanted the top down. Judy was in her teens. I was in my twenties. I was a brunette and she was blond and we had long hair. We just said "Okay!" and let him have his wish.

My sister sat on the hump. I sat in the passenger seat. We took off with my cousin driving. We had gone at least a hundred miles and were a little pass Temple, Texas. It was already getting so hot. Judy was red and her hair so wind-blown. I felt sorry for her so we changed places in the car. By the time we reached Houston, all of us looked terrible. We were sun burned. Our hair was wind-blown. We looked a mess. Our hair was so tangled that we liked to never get it fixed right. My aunt helped us get our hair combed. What a job! About eight hundred miles of wind made that trip more than memorable.

After the funeral my sister and I went back to begin our vacation in Colorado. When we were returning, we stopped again in Amarillo to call our cousin and learned that his mom and dad had driven him back to the Air Force base. They were still at a motel in Amarillo. We went to that motel and stayed the night visiting them.

The next morning we followed them back on the way to Houston. Along the way, all of a sudden, my uncle and aunt pulled off the road. I saw Aunt Faye jump out, grab a stick and start hitting at something on the side of the road. I thought she was killing a snake. We pulled in behind them and there she was, not killing a snake, but trying to wrap a tumble weed around her stick. And she did it.

I couldn't imagine why she was doing such a thing. Well, my aunt was an artist and she saw beauty in simple things. She took that tumble weed home, painted it white and made the most beautiful Christmas decoration with glittering lights inside. She was always picking up ordinary things and making them extraordinarily beautiful.

Back at home, I learned that one of my relatives needed help. It was Aunt Betty. Her husband had died and after she became a widow, she just didn't want to do anything anymore. She used to go out and dance and have fun. Now, even that didn't interest her. She just wanted to cry all the time. I thought maybe if I would stay with her, we could find something fun and interesting to do together; I thought I could *pick her up.* I took her out to stores, tried on hats, saw the sights and just did anything I thought of that she might enjoy. I told her that her husband

George would want her to continue to have fun and be happy. Nothing seemed to work.

After a while, I realized I couldn't take care of her by myself. Her great sadness was getting me sad. My Aunt Faye came to the rescue. She told her daughter, my cousin Mary Ruth, about the situation. Mary Ruth came and stayed with us. She would take Aunt Betty to the doctor and gradually those doctor visits helped her not be so sad. I learned it was good to ask for help when I was not able to do the job alone. Mary Ruth picked up my aunt's spirits and helped me keep mine. I am so grateful that I was willing to ask for help when my efforts were not enough; I was there when my family was in need and my family was there for me.

"Bear one another's burdens,
and so fulfill the law of Christ."
(Galatians 6:2)

From Past to Present

—Dolores Garcia

My mother wanted us to learn many lessons at home and at school. Where I grew up down in the Valley in Texas, there were many cultural celebrations. My mother and father were proud of their heritage and wanted us to be proud, too. Taking part in these celebrations was a part of our growing up. One of my favorites was *"Charro"* days, a southern Texas traditional celebration. The celebration was held on both sides of the border in the cities of Matamoros Mexico and Brownsville, Texas. There was so much to see, do and enjoy like Mexican *"folkloric"* dances, contests, great food and parades. Pretty ladies would dress in typical *"Charro"* outfits and ride beautiful horses in the parades. We didn't live very far from Brownsville, Texas, so we would go every year and celebrate these *"fiesta"* days. This was a family tradition and it made me proud to be Mexican-American.

We lived on a farm. My dad was the owner and we had many animals, cows for the milk, horses, goats, pigs and chickens. Our home was in Weslaco, Texas on Mile 10 and 4 ½. Mile 10 was the main street and 4 ½ was a dirt road. We had to walk from our house to Mile 10 to get the school bus because the bus in those days did not go on dirt roads.

If the weather was really bad or the roads were muddy, my dad would take us either to school or to Mile 10 to catch the school bus. He would put us in his truck and away we'd all go. There were seven of us kids. I was second oldest in our family. My brother Frank was the oldest. I had three brothers under me and two sisters very much younger. I was much older when they were born. I really grew up in the middle of my brothers and had to learn quickly how to take care of myself and to defend myself, too.

Because of my brothers I learned to play basketball, baseball, and other games with them. I really was a tomboy. My mother would buy me little dolls and dishes to play with. But, who would play with me? My brothers wouldn't play with those dolls or those dainty dishes. The three youngest children were babies. My three older brothers were my constant playmates. So, I really didn't do much girly stuff.

As we grew we helped in our home and on the farm. We'd come home from school, change into our work clothes and go to work. I would help my mother fix supper. My brothers would help my father with the animals on the farm. They would especially take out the cows. Frank, my oldest brother, because he was the oldest, got away with doing what he wanted most of the time.

At home, rules were very clear. We always knew what we needed to do. I would help wash dishes and do any job my mother had for me. The boys knew the jobs my father had for them. He'd call them and they'd just go and do whatever he'd say. If Mother or Dad told us to do something, there were no questions from us. My mother was the one who was in charge of our behavior. What she said was what we needed to do.

There was no questioning. She was very strict.

I was smart and I appreciated it when people would say, "Lolita is so smart and good." My dad would call me his *Reina*. I liked it when dad called me this, his little queen. It made me feel special. I was his little girl and he always let me know it. I was in high heaven when I was with him. His complements meant a lot to me and I was glad he was proud of me. Even when my little sisters and brothers were born, I remained my dad's *Reina*, little queen, and I loved his name for me.

We went to a Pentecostal church and loved it. We had friends there and would look forward to our Sunday school classes and services. When we were kids, church was the best place to go to have fun. I remember playing so many games. I know we prayed and sang but, the lessons didn't impress me very much as a child. Church was important to me because we went as a family and I had so much fun there with my friends. Somehow though, I must have learned the lessons taught because through the years Jesus and His church became number one to me. For so many years, God has let me serve Him in the church, teaching and leading others to Him.

Today, I am much older, wiser and live one day at a time, appreciating what my God, my church, my family and my friends mean to me. They make every day, no matter how sick I am, brighter. They bless me always. My special joy at this time is my daughter Bella who is always near when I need her. She shares her little daughter, Lunita, with me. This little grand-daughter comes over every day to visit. When her sweet voice calls me, "Grandma Telotes," she makes even my soul laugh. What blessings God shares with me in this little angel!

"...he who sows righteousness will have a sure reward. As righteous-ness leads to life..." (Proverbs 11:18 -19)

Safe in God

– Gladolia Bostick

I have two stories to share. The first happened many years ago while we were living in New Orleans, Louisiana and my daughter was going to school. This is a true story. I will never forget how God made my feet "fly" to save my daughter.

One evening my daughter who was eighteen at the time was on the Tulane Ave bus coming home from her classes at Xavier University. She was afraid because there were two guys on the bus harassing her. She thought they might try something when she would get off the bus. Normally, she would just walk home alone from the bus stop, unless it was dark and late. This evening she wasn't late and it wasn't dark. She just knew she was in danger. She knew she wasn't safe. I hung up the phone and started for the bus line.

The stop was not close to our home and I needed to walk very fast to get there on time for my daughter. My feet began to fly. Really, they didn't touch the sidewalk. I was going so fast. I looked down and I was running in plain air; my feet were not even touching the ground. God made my feet fly and I saw them. I did get to that bus line on time.

As the bus stopped, my daughter started to get off. The two men followed her. I just looked at them. They looked at me, turned around and then and there, decided not to do what they had planned. They looked afraid. I wonder, did they really see me or did they see someone else? My daughter and I walked home very aware that we were under the shelter of God's protection.

The second story happened about six years ago during Hurricane Katrina. At the time I was living alone in an area that would be totally destroyed by that hurricane. The good Lord took care of me many times and this was another time He really was with me. I was about seventy-five years old and He helped me do what I could have never done by myself.

I had gone to church that morning and by the time I got home it started raining. I didn't know it was going to be so bad. I didn't know everyone was leaving. I went into my house. It rained so hard. Soon the water was very high. It was covering every-thing. I put some food in a little sack, took it with me and climbed a tree next to my house.

After I got in that tree, I don't know how I did it, but I jumped on to the roof of my house. I had something white with me and a little food. It was very hot there. I would move around and try to sit in the shade of the chimney during the day. At night, when it got cool, I would change and get on the other side of the chimney. After three days and three nights a man in a helicopter came and found me. He lowered something like a hammock for me. I got in it and they carried me to a safe place.

No one knew where I was. My family really thought I was dead. I wasn't sure if they were alive either. I had no idea if anyone would ever find me. I was in a school in Thibodaux, Louisiana for a while. Everyone was very nice to me there. Some ladies brought me clothes and took me out to eat. I wrote my nickname on a blackboard so they could look for my family. I had put "Sugar Babe" because that's what everyone called me. One of my cousins found out where I was and soon my family found me. I don't really know how everything happened in those days. We all were in different places. After a while we found each other and my daughter and I moved to Houston, Texas.

So many people died in Katrina. The good Lord blessed me and my family, saved us in danger and brought us safely back together.

"For, He shall give His angels charge over you, To keep you in all your ways. In their hands

they shall bear you up, Lest you dash your foot against a stone."
(Psalm 91:11-12)

Young and in love, Guy and Naomi Worsham

Crashing a Party

– Guy Worsham

A ll of my life God honored me
with His blessings. My family

moved from the country to Orange, Texas after the war broke out. There I went to Lutcher Stark High School. After graduation I planned on attending the University of Houston. I checked it out and when I didn't have enough money to register, I worked for a year to earn what I needed. Finally, I was ready and able to register as a college student. That year in the fall of 1948, I was seventeen and God was still in the business of blessing me as I continued to honor Him.

I was proficient in typing and shorthand but in order to get my degree to teach business classes in high school, which was the plan I had in mind, I needed to have shorthand and typing on my transcript. Well, let me tell you how God got busy this time sending another miracle my way.

The registrar came in and told me that since I was already proficient in those two areas of typing and shorthand would I consider teaching those courses to the freshmen and sophomore classes because a teacher had not been hired yet. Here, I arrived to become a student. God came ahead of me and I was being offered a chance to be a professor at the age of seventeen, a professor teaching what I had already mastered. God again stepped in turning my life around. What an honor! I could do nothing but honor Him back and accept this position with confidence. I was given all the privileges allotted to any professor in that University of Houston, even a private lunch room, keys and complete access to the school.

During these days in Houston I decided to visit a little Assembly of God Church on the north side. I wanted to check out the girls there. I had been told by my brother and sister-in-law to come over. They said the pastor had a very attractive daughter. I went over there and found out she was only fifteen years old and the pastor wouldn't let her date unless she went with another friend. I made friends with her best friend Dora and asked her mother if

I could take her out for a coke after class. Dora's mother agreed as long as I would ask the pastor's daughter to go along, too. That was exactly what I had hoped. Naomi did come along with Dora and me and that made the coke date ever so sweet.

There were twelve boys and two girls in that Sunday school class, so I didn't think I had a chance. I knew what I wanted and I wouldn't give up. God made me persistent for a reason. The pastor's daughter soon would be sixteen and I learned one of the other young men in class was giving her a birthday party. I knew I had to take action. Even though I had not been personally invited, Naomi Ruth Kent was going to be sixteen and I was determined I would be there to celebrate with her.

I thought to myself and said, "Self, you had better make your move." I decided I would just go to that party and very politely, crash it. I got in my 1939 Ford and I just eased over there. I walked in like I was invited. Everybody was playing that game called, "Knock." That's when all the girls get in a room and close the door. The guys get to knock a number of times on the door. If that girl chose the number knocked, she walks out of the room and the lucky guy gets to walk her around the block.

When I walked in, the game hadn't started yet. I just said, "Oh, I'll be the first," and went to the door.

"Knock-knock-knock!" went my hand very carefully. Somewhere I had heard Naomi say her favorite number was three. And, today it still is. I knocked on that door three times and when the door opened and she came out, you couldn't touch me with a forty foot pole.

I said, "Thank you, Jesus! My prayers have been answered." I took that pretty little girl directly to my 39 Ford, cranked it up and we took off and never walked around that block. That was April 30 of 1950. On July 29, 1950, three months later, we were married. It's been that way sixty-two, now going on sixty-three years. I have never forgotten how to knock on my sweet lady's door.

"Ask, and it will be given to you; seek, and you will find; knock, and it will be opened to you."
(Matthew 7:7)

Singing

— Ilse Miller

S inging was my favorite thing to do. When I was twelve or thirteen I took part in a talent show and sang, "Somewhere over the Rainbow." I think my parents had just arrived in time and were looking for a place to sit. They came rushing into the auditorium. I was excited to perform and they were excited to see and hear me. In that hurried moment my mother lost one of the earrings she was wearing. They did get to hear me sing my song, but in the excitement, my mother never found her lost earring. After the talent show, my parents went to a dance at my dad's college. My mother was probably the only lady there wearing just one earring.

Through the years, I loved to sing more and more. I would sing whenever I had the opportunity. I was in the choir and had a good voice. I was an alto and would sing the harmony part in our songs. When I was in high school, I got to be a tenor because all the boys' voices were changing and they could only sing those low notes. They needed me as a tenor and I loved it because tenors sing the melodies.

There was a special singing group that performed all around town. I sang tenor in that little group for a long time. Basically, we went to youth clubs in the area. We participated in choral festivals where all the school choirs got together, competed and performed. At this time I started singing again the harmony part as an alto. I enjoyed this so very much.

Singing is and always has been such a blessing for me. I have always appreciated this wonderful gift in my life. When I sing, the songs come from my heart. When I sing to God, these songs are prayers from my very soul. Songs to me are so special. Singing has always been a way to speak from my heart. And, it has been a most pleasant joyful way for sure!

"Make melody to Him with an instrument of ten strings. Sing to Him a new song." (Psalms 33:2-3)

Messy and Sweet

– Ellinor Nieto

When I was about ten years old, I was in a school play. I was dressed as a gypsy for my part. My hair was very long and my grandma would braid it so nicely. In the play there was a princess and a gypsy, me. The princess was like Snow White with a beautiful dress and she was so clean and pretty.

A group from a theater came to our school to help us get ready for our play. They dressed us and made us look the part we were playing. They even put makeup on our faces. When I arrived at school for the play, I was clean and my hair was braided so beautifully.

The people who were there to get us ready made some changes in my appearance. I guess I looked too nice for the part of that gypsy. They unbraided my hair and made it messy even putting ashes in it and on my dress, too. I looked a sight. I peeked through the curtains and saw my grandma in the first row. I knew she would have her eyes on me when I appeared on stage. I also knew she probably wouldn't like the way I looked now.

You can imagine what happened after the play. My grandma looked so surprised when she saw me. She said, "What did you do? I gave you a bath and made you so clean and beautiful. What happened? How did you get so dirty?" She did not understand that I had to look this way for the part and that real theater people fixed me this way.

The princess was so beautiful and my grandmother did not understand why I had to look so bad with my dress of rags and dirty hair. I was singing in the forest. The princess and her court were coming home to the castle. The princess said, "You cannot sing in the forest. It belongs to me." I said to her, "It belongs to everyone and you cannot tell me to not sing. It is my home, too." The princess said, "Get out of my forest. I don't want to see you here anymore."

The princess was holding a big yellow apple in her hand. I wasn't really listening to what she was saying to me. I was looking at that apple. I said to myself, "I haven't eaten all day long." So, I said "Princess, will you come a little bit closer to me?" I got her hand and took a big bite out of her apple. She started crying so I said, "Do not cry because I did not take the whole apple, but if you keep on crying, I will eat all of it."

My grandma let me know what she thought about my dirty clothes, messy hair and how I treated that princess. She said, "That's not right. I taught you better than that. I didn't bring you up to steal apples from other little girls." I don't think she knew that I was acting.

"And behold, I am coming quickly, and My reward is with Me, to give to everyone according to his work."
(Revelations 22: 12)

Bella and Mack with their two little girls Linda and Brenda

Love Endures

– Bella Vedros

I remember when we went to school. We had to walk about a mile to get there. We missed a lot of days because my papa didn't have a car and on bad days there was no way to get us to school. Other children walked, too and had the same problem during those bad weather days. There were no school buses for us in those days.

On the way to school it was not unusual to carry a container of milk for an older lady who lived along the way. We would take that container from our mother and bring it to this neighbor as we walked the path to school.

Our school was small. I remember it had three classrooms. Our school only went to seventh grade. I didn't go to high school because the high school was too far to walk. We also needed to help work in the fields. Most of our neighbors didn't have a car when I was growing up either. Many others didn't get to go to high school because they, too, were needed at home.

My mama was always home doing the cooking, the washing and everything that needed to be done to keep our home nice and us safe. During the day Papa would be working hard on the farm. I would help Mama with the work when I was home. We all helped around the house and farm. My oldest brother Wiltz when he was in his twenties joined the service and went to war. We missed him when he left and it broke our hearts when we learned he died so far away from home. The conditions were so bad over there that he caught malaria and later pneumonia and died April 12, 1945.

Everyone was so sad when they brought his body back home three years later in September, 1948. My mama and papa bought a family plot in Lock Port, Louisiana. My brother Wiltz was our first family member buried there. We all felt his loss greatly.

During the war time I worked in a sugar mill. A lot of the men went to service so the women went to work to help pay for expenses. Many of my friends worked at the factory. It is a funny thing because I met my husband at that factory. He didn't really work at the factory. He was a carpenter and built things for the factory. God must have wanted us to meet because it just happened that he came there when I was there. I still laugh a little when I think about it. We just met each other and liked each other right away.

After a while Mack came to the house to meet my mama and papa. I was twenty-nine when we married. Mack was 16 years older. In those days age didn't matter much. He asked me to marry him. I said "Yes." When we got married we moved to Mathews, Louisiana not far from the sugar cane factory.

Mack had three children from his first wife who had died shortly after her last baby boy, Ernest, was born. His daughter, Rita, dropped out of school when her mother died to take care of the house, her father and her two brothers. It must have been hard on her since she was so young. She just stepped in caring for the family as her mother would have done. She was a very brave little girl. By the time I met Mack, Rita was quite grown up as she welcomed me as the new wife in this beautiful family. About a year after I married Mack, Rita herself found her own sweetheart and married.

Later, my husband and I had two little girls. When Ernest was twelve years old, his first new little sister Brenda was born. He was fourteen when Linda came along. He loved his new position as older brother to the both of them and it was good having him around to help care for our little girls. He was their big brother and very proud of it.

Today, I am ninety-six years old. This sweet son, Ernest, who called me Mama from the very beginning, is seventy-seven. His visits still mean the world to me. His older brother and sister have since gone to heaven. My husband's son-in-law, sister-in-law, and all his relatives still living, visit me. It is nice knowing we keep up with each other even today with love and care. Remembering the day I became a wife and a mama in this sweet family makes me smile.

I love my family and all of my relatives. When I said, "Yes" to Mack Vedros so many years ago, little did I realize I would have such a wonderful and long life, rich in ways that cannot be counted with such a huge family and many treasured memories.

"Love…bears all things, believes all things, hopes all things, endures all things. Love never fails." (1 Corinthians 13:4, 7-8)

Honeymoon on Wheels

– Louise E.

Being eighty-four I don't think I remember too much. Of all my memories, the one that stands out to me most is my honeymoon. My husband and I had a simple wedding. His family was there and my family was there. We didn't need a lot of people. We just needed each other. I don't remember exactly how we met. I do remember he was with two friends. He came to see me in a car with those two friends. They had dates and I was his date.

When we married, we both were working, so our honeymoon had to be short. We decided to make it a traveling honeymoon. We took about a week and a half and just drove looking at the many sights. We went through south west Texas, New Mexico and Colorado. We stayed at motels along the way and really enjoyed so much beauty in our country.

Carlsbad Caverns in New Mexico is one of the places I really remember. It was cool and very beautiful down in those caves. I had never seen anything like that before. We both enjoyed relaxing in this National Park and seeing the beauty created through the years.

Another sight that was so glorious was Pikes Peak in Colorado. Those mountains were majestic and I had never seen anything so grand in my home town. Brownsville, Texas where I lived didn't even have small hills.

When we got back home we had many memories to treasure. We returned to work and enjoyed sharing our travels with our family and friends. We felt like we had become fancy travelers and had such a great time celebrating our honeymoon in three states on the road.

"He has made everything beautiful in its time." (Ecclesiastes 3:11)

A Green Thumb

— Sanny Laxton

When my daddy came out of the hospital I moved in to help him and my mother. I would help work in the yard and in the house. One day I went to the store and saw the tomatoes were green and they cost $3.00. I thought, "There's no way I am going to pay that much for green tomatoes." So I went and bought tomato plants and other vegetables and planted them in my flower garden.

I learned how to use those landscaping boards and soon was planting other gardens with the vegetables we wanted. We also had planted two peach trees, two pecan trees and two beautiful red bud trees. I remembered that my mom threw ashes around our peach trees when I was a little girl, so I started throwing ashes around the trees, too. I put fertilizer around them, too. I heard on the radio that you're supposed to trim the tops of the peach trees to make the peaches larger. I used limb cutters and trimmed the tops of my trees and the peaches did grow huge.

My dad liked to sit on the porch and look at the trees and the garden. He'd see those peaches and say, "I think there are some peaches ready to be picked." I'd go pick those peaches and bring them in to make a milk shake with my own special recipe." I'd put peaches in the blender, a cup of milk for me, ensure for my daddy, brown sugar, oatmeal and ice cubes. That was our favorite summer drink. My daddy liked it too much. The doctor said I needed to start giving him less. He was gaining too much weight.

Some of the other vegetables besides tomatoes were sweet potatoes, corn and pumpkins. When I would cut the corn, the sweet potatoes and pumpkins would grow quickly. My dad would be looking out of the kitchen window, see a pumpkin and say, "I sure could use a pumpkin pie." I'd go out, get a pumpkin and make a pumpkin pie for him. When the pumpkins were big, I'd make two pumpkin pies.

During those years of helping my dad and growing our garden, I read many books on gardening and watched a gardening show on TV. My dad even listened to one on the radio. Our garden kept us busy, working, watching, listening and eating.

"And he who reaps receives wages, and gathers fruit for eternal life, that both he who sows and he who reaps may rejoice together."
(John 4:36)

Paulette holding her Bonnie Braids doll

Dolls Hidden and Honored

—Paulette Meeks

W hen I was growing up, I always liked dolls. My mom and dad always gave my sisters and me a doll for Christmas. My doll was my favorite present and I really took care of her.

One year, when I was old enough to read the comics in the newspaper, my favorite was the one about Dick Tracy. I don't know if I thought much about him but I fell in love with his baby. Her name was Bonnie Braids and the year she became *famous,* of course a doll came out in her honor. It was the rage that Christmas. All of my girlfriends in school wanted this little doll and so did I. I probably told my grandmother about this wish of mine every day because she got me one.

Grandma had carefully wrapped it and put it in a closet hidden from me until Christmas. The problem was when I would visit her, which was nearly every day, Bonnie Braids and I would spend time together. I would go to that closet, find that gift, un-wrap it, look at that sweet little rubber baby doll with big blue eyes and love her to pieces. She had two golden braids, one coming out of the top of each side of that little head and she was just too cute. I'd look into her eyes, hug, kiss her and ever so quietly place her back in that box. Then, I would re-wrap grandma's gift for me and put it back in its hiding place.

Weeks later at the Christmas party, I carefully opened that present (which probably showed signs of many previous un-wrappings). No doubt I "oohed!" and acted surprised as I showed excitement and contentment at this cherished gift. Probably my grandmother had a good silent laugh since she must have realized my Bonnie Braids wasn't as new to me as I pretended. I was young and she was wise and so accepting of my childish actions. I think she realized my real lack of surprise did not take away my appreciation for her.

When I was eight or nine years old, I started creating my own little dolls with clothespins, socks, cardboard, material scraps, spools, yarn, and even egg shells. I would work really hard on these creations and thought they were beautiful.

Looking back now, I realize they probably didn't really have that great of an appearance. But, I loved them and the best thing was my grandmother let me know they were beautiful to her. She even let me put them in a special place in her china closet. She took my little creations and placed them right by her finest treasures and best china.

To this day, the appreciation my grandmother had for me and her thoughtfulness makes me grateful for her quiet way of teaching me the importance of letting others know, especially young children in my life, that they and all of their dreams are important to me, too.

*"Whoever receives one little child
like this in My name, receives Me."
(Matthew 18:5)*

Vacation in Hawaii

—Mary Gene Hortman

P ete was an accountant and had just moved to Houston from Fort Worth. He was renting a room some place on Hines Boulevard in Houston. Since Pete was new in town, he didn't know many people. Both he and I shared a mutual friend. This friend, Billy had invited me to be a date of another friend of his. Pete was invited to come along for the evening. It makes me be in awe how God's plan brings lives together.

Billy called asking me if I would be a date for a friend of his. We went to a club, Billy, my date, Pete his new friend, and me. Well, my date got quite drunk and Billy drove him home. I sat in the back seat with my date. Billy and Pete were in the front. After my date was dropped off at his home, Pete jumped in the back seat with me. And, that's how it all began. We hit it off immediately.

We dated for six months and fell in love. Since this happened in the fifties during the draft, my Pete was drafted. We married before he was sent on his first assignment. He came from California and wore his Army dress suit at our wedding. He was very handsome. We were so much in love. We knew his being away would be very hard. We didn't know where he would be sent and we didn't know how long we would be apart.

Pete returned to California and waited for his deployment. What a great day it was when that call came. He would be stationed in Hawaii and as soon as he could, he would send for me. Three long months followed. He saved his money, rented a small apartment off the base in Honolulu, and called for me to come be with him.

The day for my departure from Houston came. I remember I had on a beautiful blue suit and a hat, too. My mother and father brought me to the airport and took lots of pictures of me. I flew from Houston to California and then to Honolulu, Hawaii. I was so excited. My husband and I would finally be together.

Pete met me when that plane landed. I remember being so happy when I saw him there. He put those festive Hawaiian lays on me and took me straight from the airport to our apartment. I remember the shrubbery was so tropical and those magnificent flowers of so many colors. My whole world was filled with all the colors of the rainbow. I couldn't get over it.

Our apartment was small. The bed would fold up into the wall and we had a small kitchen. It was heaven to us. It was our own place, our home. In that little part of heaven I became pregnant and had my first son, Peter Morgan. He was born in the Honolulu Army hospital and was named after my husband and my father.

We lived in Honolulu for fifteen months. We would go all around that Island enjoying its tropical beauty and glimmering sea. The waters were always so blue. The surf would come in and we would just sun bathe hearing the soothing sounds and seeing the beautiful sites. I always had a nice suntan. It was like a very wonderful long vacation for me. We didn't have a lot of money, but we didn't need it to be happy. We were newly married and we had each other. We had all we needed.

"How much better… wisdom than gold! And … understanding … rather than silver." (Proverbs 16:16)

Protect and Comfort

−Dorothy Wiggins

When my mother was two years old, her mother died. My great grandmother raised her. Great-grandmother was a prayer warrior, a pillar of faith in our family. If she said something, you could mark it down.

My grandfather had the first car in our family. When we would go to church, he'd pack that car as full as it could get with as many family members as possible. I don't know what model it was. I just know it could hold a lot of people. One time we were all packed in and running late to church. It was beginning to get dark. We were nearing the train tracks. In those days there were no arms or lights to protect cars crossing at railroad tracks. Grandpa didn't realize a train was right there coming fast toward the crossing. Just as our car arrived at those tracks, so did the train. My great-grandmother in the back seat screamed, "Jesus!" Grand-daddy stopped the car within inches of being hit by that train.

After the train went by, everybody was so quiet. They just sat there. From the back seat Granny said,

"Children, did you all see that arm come between us and that train?" We all said, "Granny, we didn't see any arm at all." A lot of times we don't see. But you can be sure, it is always there, ready to take care of us and keep us from danger.

Another incident of God's forever care comes to mind. My husband and I bought a new house in the city of Spring, Texas. It was much larger than the first house we had purchased. Our son was five years old and he wasn't used to having much room to run. He was so excited and began to run all around in our new den. He was running fast and having a ball. I said, "Be careful! You're going to hurt yourself." But, being five, his excitement was without fear and there was just so much room.

A big brick hearth stuck out in the den. As he ran by it, he caught his little toe and knocked the toenail completely off. I was watching him when it happened and he didn't cry or even say a word. He just stood there looking as white as a sheet. I didn't even think about my new carpet. That didn't enter my head. Blood was squirting everywhere.

I ran, grabbed him up in my arms, and thought he was in shock. I shouted, "Baby, cry, cry. It's got to hurt!" I realized I needed to stop the bleeding. I put him on top of the cabinet and ran cold water over his foot trying to stop the flow of blood. I wanted my baby to know I was there for him and would do everything I could to help him be alright and out of pain. And you know what? That's exactly how the Lord treats us.

"As one whom his mother comforts, So I will comfort you."
(Isaiah 66:13)

The first day of our 51 ½ wonderful years together

It's a Boy

—Joyce Green Jones (Lady J)

Last week all of my family and I were in Austin with my daughter, Patti and her family. Last year she said, "We always come to Houston for Christmas. Have you ever thought of coming to Austin to celebrate?" Her three girls are married now and have their families there. They would always travel to be with us. So this year we did the traveling.

We all went to Austin and had a wonderful time…all of us together.

I am just so blessed and thank the Lord for everything.

Being together with family always brings good memories to me. God has given me such a beautiful life. I couldn't have been married to a more wonderful man than Franklin G Jones. God gave us fifty-one and a half years together. That was a miracle, too! The Lord worked all that out for us. I don't know why I am so blessed…I just know I definitely am.

The way the Lord works things out is just a miracle! When we moved to Houston, Daddy rented a house. Then he said, "That's just throwing money away. We're going to buy a house." So he bought a house in Denver-Harbor Addition for $1400.

It was a two-bedroom house for two parents and four children. We moved in May 5, 1940 and three days later, May 8th, my baby brother was born in the front bedroom of that house.

The neighbors who lived next door to us were a couple who didn't have any children. They were the Wilsons. Mrs. Wilson was related to Dorothy Jones who was married to Ira Jones. When I was growing up, there were five or six Pentecostal churches in Houston. We would have fellowship meetings and youth rallies and were acquainted with members in those churches. Ira Jones was one of the pastors.

The Joneses had a son named Franklin. He was right in the middle of thirteen kids. After we had grown up, Mrs. Wilson always wanted Franklin and me to get together. Franklin had come to our house for parties with his friends so we did know each other.

When I was twenty-one and had just come home from work one day, there was Mrs. Wilson at the back fence, ready to tell me something. Though she didn't have children of her own, she managed to keep busy with the Green family and their children. She was watching through her blinds and saw me drive up. She came out of the back door and met me at the fence, saying, "Joyce, Franklin's home on leave." (He had joined the Navy.) I said, "Oh, he is. That's good."

I walked in the house and my mom and dad were there. I told them, "Mrs. Wilson let me know that Franklin Jones is home on leave…A lot of good that's going to do me!"

That day I had picked up sheet music to play for my cousin's wedding, so I went to the piano in the living room to practice. About that time the phone rang and my daddy answered it. Then, he called loudly to me in the other room, "Joyce, telephone! It's a boy." I responded, "Oh, Dad, don't say that!"

It was Franklin Jones. His first words to me were, "It's a boy." He wanted to take me on a date. Guess where we went. Our first date was to a fellowship meeting over at Brother Lambert's Church. That was the beginning.

I kept telling myself, "You're not going to fall for this handsome guy. He's a sailor…he will love you and leave you." All the time I was telling myself not to, I was falling head over heels! Back in my mind I always wanted to date him. The Lord worked it out and we both knew right off that we were meant for each other. This was in the spring of 1955 and we began writing each other and made occasional long distance phone calls.

Frank was stationed on a ship after his training…the U.S.S. St. Paul…

and, he had one more overseas trip to make. The ship was docked in California. That spring I had bought a brand new 1955 Ford. My dad had some cousins living in California and he said, "If you'll furnish the car, I'll furnish the gas and we'll go to California this summer." We had a deal! We arrived there the week before Frank had to go back overseas. We had a wonderful time...we became officially engaged.

This is funny and it is true. My parents and I were staying in a motel and Frank did not have duty on the weekend, so he spent one night with us in the motel. He slept with my dad and I slept with my mom. He would always tease me saying, "I slept with your daddy before I slept with you."

When he returned home, we were married a month later on April 28, 1956. We had such a wonderful love story all through the years. God has blessed me with many miracles. Our love story is one I hold most dear.

"Love never fails." (1 Corinthians 13:8)

Florida Surprise

−A. H.

I n 1941, an aunt of mine sent me a special gift for graduation from high school. It was a trip for my little sister and me. We were going to visit her in Florida for the summer. She and my uncle had moved out there from Chicago. She sent us tickets for a bus trip to Miami. We packed fruit, sandwiches, drinks and treats and enjoyed two days traveling from our home in El Paso, Texas to Miami, Florida.

It was the best trip we ever had. We were all by ourselves and spent two days and two nights on that bus. The bus driver would make sure we were safe at the different stops because at that time it was not unusual for young girls by themselves to be kidnapped. He made sure that wouldn't happen to us.

When we arrived in Florida, my uncle was there to meet us. He took us to his home and we got to stay the whole three months in that lovely place with my aunt and him. It was wonderful. We even went on a bus to Orlando to visit another aunt and went shopping in fancy stores. We did things we never got to do at home. Goodness, we even went to

Disney World. It was fascinating for us. We had never seen anything like that before.

It so happened that my aunt had a good friend who had a nephew visiting at that time. He arrived in Miami the same day my sister and I arrived. He had gone there to visit his aunt while we had gone to visit ours. Both of our aunts worked at the same store.

His aunt found out that I had just arrived and thought it would be nice if we met each other. She said, "I have a nephew that you need to meet." God surely had His plans. Who would have thought this meeting could happen like this? He was my age and so nice.

He would come to the house in a fancy car and take my sister and me to the beach or to the parks and we'd spend the day having a picnic, walking on the white sandy shore, seeing the beauty of that Atlantic Ocean and those graceful sea-gulls flying over the water. We would always pack a delicious lunch and he'd even bring extra fruit, candy or cakes. We did this just about every weekend for three months.

When summer was over, my sister and I returned home. She had to go to school and I watched over and cared for her and my dad. I didn't even think about that boy I had met in Florida. To be honest I thought he probably forgot me, too.

During that year we never called or wrote to each other. We didn't even know each other's address.

A year later, I decided to go back and live with my aunt in Miami. When I returned, my gentleman friend was there and I learned he hadn't forgotten me at all and he hoped I hadn't forgotten him either.

"To everything there is a season,
A time for every purpose under
heaven…and A time to love."
(Ecclesiastes 3:1, 8)

God Sees More

— Veronica Morris

I was born with cerebral palsy and learned to use a wheel chair when I was two or three years old. There were many things I missed as a child. When I think back, the first memory that comes to my mind happened while I was in high school. I was a junior. I had gone to my junior-senior prom. Since I was in a wheel chair, I didn't go to dances like most kids my age, but

I had no intention of missing my junior-senior prom.

Sometimes kids made fun of me because I couldn't do things that they could do. It hurt my feelings a lot. I was just like them. They didn't see that. They let me know so often that to them I was an invalid and when I attempted to do something that might be a challenge to me physically, some even laughed at me. They didn't really see me for who I was. I know many of the other kids couldn't even imagine why I would want to go to the junior-senior prom. I remember one girl saying, "Why are you going? How can you dance in a wheelchair?"

When I couldn't do normal things or wasn't even allowed to try, it made me sad. You know, I really wanted to do everything they did. I wanted at least, the chance to try. I wanted people to see me for the person I was. My heart could dance, even if my feet couldn't. And I loved music. So, I went to that dance. Some girls near me were giggling. I don't know why. Some let me know they were laughing at me. I was not going to give up. I wore my beautiful yellow dress. My hair was fixed up in a bun and I wore black dress shoes. I had my glasses on and I was beautiful.

A young boy came over to me, smiled and said, "Would you like to dance?" to me. Wow! Someone else saw the real me. They were playing the song from REO Speedway, "I can't stop this feeling anymore." He just took my wheel chair and moved me ever so gently on that dance floor. That was such a happy moment for me. As this young boy, Robert danced with me I felt as free as a lovely bird. I will never forget it. After that dance, the girls who had laughed at me earlier were clapping for me and they apologized for how they had treated me. God had let them see, I was not an invalid; I was very valid to Him. God let them see and me, too, through the eyes of young Robert, that I was someone He values very much and He let me glow in that moment.

"I can do all things through Christ who strengthens me… And my God shall supply all your need according to His riches in glory by Christ Jesus." (Philippians 4:13-19)

George, Mary, baby Sarah, Sally and Wilhelmina before trip

Dad's Trip up North

—Sarah Duplease

My father always wanted to have twelve children. He didn't get his wish, but he did have seven and we all lived together with Mom and him in Santa Rosa, Texas. He worked so hard to take care of us even when he was very sick. I think he realized how sick he was and decided to go visit relatives, his brothers and sisters in Massachusetts. I think he knew he was dying and wanted to tell them good-bye.

He had an old big black Packard that he had driven for many years. We all packed into that car with Mom and Dad and started on the long journey. I am sure Dad was very tired. He wouldn't let Mom drive because she was taking care of the babies. Even with TB he still felt strong enough to make that long drive.

We were heading east, going through Tennessee and it was not just a dark night but a very foggy dark night. Dad stopped the car because the visibility was so bad, he could not see the road at all. He put his foot down out of the car and realized there was nothing there, no dirt, no road, no nothing. So, he put his foot back in the car very slowly and asked Mom to see if it was safer on her side of the car. She got out carefully with no problem. She found the white line that marked the outside of the road easily. She walked ahead of the car staying on the white line. My dad drove the car ever so slowly behind her.

The roads in Tennessee wind around hills and mountains and have cliff areas where a car could accidentally drive off. I think we passed at least one very closely that night. We went through many dangerous and dark tunnels that night, too. We went through tunnel after tunnel after tunnel. It was a scary trip for sure. I was about four years old and I still remember it.

We arrived in New York and right there in Times Square our car broke down. I have no idea where Dad put the car because we all went to a hotel in New York to spend the night. I remember my mom saying, "We're going to have soup tonight and do not break your crackers in the soup." We were going to eat in a restaurant and she wanted us to be right and proper.

My dad called his family and his two brothers-in-law. My Uncle George and Uncle Henry came to New York the next day to help out. One of them drove my mother and us seven kids to Massachusetts to be with family. The other uncle stayed and helped Dad fix the car. My dad was a mechanic and the help of his brother-in-law was a real support at this time, especially after that long trip. They both fixed the car and drove to Massachusetts where we were.

We stayed and visited for a while with all the relatives. Dad got to see his brothers and sisters and we made friends with new family members. It was good my dad chose to make the trip while he was still well enough and we were glad to meet so many new aunts, uncles, and cousins. We learned we had family in New York, Massachusetts, Connecticut, New Hampshire, Pennsylvania and Canada. We had many relatives in many places who loved us very much.

"For You are my hope, O Lord, God. You are my trust from my youth." (Psalm 71:5)

That Date

— Ellinor Nieto

L et me tell you of my first date with the love of my life, my Hector. At the time I met him, I wasn't too anxious to date anyone I didn't know. I trusted a friend I had grown to know and appreciate, Mrs. Cole, my landlady. I let her meet Hector first and waited for her impression. After meeting him she said with confidence, "He's okay. You can go."

We left in Hector's shiny red MG. We were driving up to the Queens Borough Bridge which leads to Manhattan from Queens. It started drizzling. He stopped the car, got out and looked for a piece of cloth. I started wondering what in the world was I supposed to do now. Should I call for a taxi?

I was standing in my new dress and heels in the drizzling rain and he was wiping off his red MG. I started thinking to myself, "What a guy I have now. Am I really a winner here?" So we got back in the car and continued driving until we met up with Sally and her date at the restaurant.

Hector ordered a big steak and Sally and her date did the same. I thought to myself if Hector ordered that big steak he would not have enough money to pay for me so I ordered beef stew. The waiter looked at me with a look that said, "Hey lady! What's with you ordering beef stew when all the others are going to have a big steak?" I think he thought I was sick or something.

After our meal we said, "Good-bye," to Sally and her friend and Hector drove me back home in his red MG. Mrs. Cole was waiting at the door to see if everything was right. I just shook his hand and thanked Hector for the nice evening and went into the house.

The next morning, when I came home from work, Mrs. Cole was there waiting for me and said, "He sent a big bouquet of flowers." I said maybe they were for her. She said, "No, no, no! They are for you. The card says they are for you." He thanked me for the lovely evening. Now, I figured he was getting nice there. Maybe I was more important than his car.

Mrs. Cole left for Miami and stayed for about a six-week visit. She trusted me completely to care for the house while she was away. Hector and I continued dating at least twice a week after our first date. I never let him into the house while my landlady was away. It was not my house and I was responsible for it. So, Hector and I always went to restaurants or friends' homes. Since the house belonged to Mrs. Cole, we didn't feel it was right to party or date there.

Hector and I met on June 6, 1951. I changed jobs and started working in the office of Lufthansa Airlines. We continued dating and going to many parties. Hector liked parties. He surprised me with a birthday party for me on September 10, 1954. What a surprise party that was! There were many friends there. All of a sudden, everything got quiet. Hector took my hand and he said, "I would like to give you my heart and my ring." We were engaged.

"Pleasant words are like a honeycomb, Sweetness to the soul and health to the bones."
(Proverbs16:24)

Healing Warmth

—Berta Hinojosa

Something happened to me when I was thirty-eight years old and I will never forget it. Today I still recall the miracle of that special moment. I had just learned from my doctor that I had cancer. I returned home and was praying, asking God to help me. I dozed off and while I slept I had a dream.

The following are parts of the dream that still touch my soul today. I saw myself going through a passage. In front of me was a brilliant beautiful light. It looked like the light was shaping into a figure, but I couldn't clearly see it. It was so bright. I was talking with that light, telling of my pain, asking to be healed.

I looked at the light and pleaded for help. I couldn't take the pain I was in. I asked to be healed again. I looked into the light and felt such warmth going through my whole body. I had never felt anything like this before. I asked, "What are you? Who are you?" I heard this response, "I am the son in your heart." I did not know what that meant. I just know I had been given peace in that response.

I awoke and that warm peace still filled my body.

Weeks and months passed. I took medication that I was given by the doctor. During that time I became pregnant and didn't know it. When I went to the doctor, she told me I was two months pregnant. I was surprised. We had three daughters and because I had been ill, my husband and I had not planned on having any more children at that time. I did not experience any morning sickness with my daughters so I didn't know the "illness" I was going through at this time was actually morning sickness.

The doctor told me that because of the medication she had given me, the baby I was carrying would be born severely handicapped. She wanted me to have an abortion. She said the baby would be mongoloid or I would not be able to carry it to full term. I decided I would not get an abortion. My morning sickness continued for five months, but I was determined to remain strong and do everything I could to keep that baby alive. I did my best. Though I tried hard, after five months, I did have a miscarriage. It turned out I was not just carrying one baby. I was carrying twin boys and to my great sadness, I did lose the both of them.

The doctor said if it hadn't been for the miscarriage of these two boys, a tumor that was in me would not have been discovered on time. When they had to take the babies from me, the tumor was found and removed. My doctor said that this tumor had been the cause of the cancer that was destroying my health.

I remembered that dream I had of the light and that voice that described itself as the "son in my heart." Maybe Jesus, the Son in my heart had let me carry these little sons of my heart blessed by Him to be that warm blessing to heal my body. I believe God let these little angels, these babies within me, heal my life. One day I will see and hug these two little sons I never got to know. I will tell them, "I love you two, who loved me first."

"...those who know Your name will put their trust in You; For You, Lord, have not forsaken those who seek You." (Psalm 9:10)

Bill smiling in the midst of so many flowers.

Eyes of His Soul

— Paulette Meeks

My husband and I became cruising buddies. When we were young neither of us thought much about traveling just to see places. We both had traveled many places mostly on short vacations or to visit or help others. We had never even thought about traveling just for the fun of it or simply, just for ourselves.

When we became older seasoned citizens, seniors, as we liked to call ourselves, we caught a "bug" that made us just want to have fun and see everything beautiful we possibly could. And thus we became hooked on cruising any and every place possible.

In the beginning, we just expected to take it easy and enjoy being on the vast oceans of our world. We soon learned that God's beauty went beyond even the horizons we saw on the so very blue waters. As soon as we would come home from a cruise, my sweet husband would already be planning for our next one.

He wanted to go to the Island of Martinque. He knew the history of this island and it fascinated him. We found a cruise that went there once a year and we were on their next list of passengers. We had found that though the island had been destroyed years ago by a volcano, now it was one of the rarest beauties with a variety of flowers than could not be counted. One of our guides told us that as soon as they had a count, someone would find a new variety or species.

With cameras in hand we docked at Martinque, the Island of Flowers, as it is called. We were so enthralled with the beauty all around us that we literally got lost in the garden and separated from our guided group. I was taking a picture of Bill taking pictures. All of a sudden he looked at me and sat down on the ground. I could tell by his face he was frightened and could not breathe.

I went to him, held on to him, and called for help. Soon I realized no one spoke English. Everyone around us spoke French. I could see our ship in the distance and I could see me losing the love of my life so far away from home at that moment.

As a child I knew French, a little at least. Now all languages escaped me. Then, without even thinking God gave me courage to blurt out whatever I needed in French and a young girl responded telling me clearly she was going for help. God's love and grace has no language barriers. Those words coming from me were part one of a miracle. Understanding the girl was another. I sat next to my sweetie and prayed right there on the ground with him.

Then God blessed us with a moment of such gentleness and healing. Bill was wearing a baseball cap. He turned his cap on his head around like a little kid and looked me in the eyes and grinned. He made me laugh. He really had the look of an impish little boy and his eyes held a smile only heaven could explain. I heard in my heart "All is well!" I knew God had renewed his body and soul and mine, too. I didn't take a picture of his face at that moment and I didn't need to. It is a look into his soul and I will never forget it. What a treasured memory that will always be!

"I will lift up my eyes to the hills–
From whence comes my help?"
(Psalms 121:1)

What I Never Expected

—Beth Christian

When I was fifteen my teacher, Miss Wylie would do a lot of things with me. One day she came to my house and picked me up to go shopping with her. We went to craft stores because we both liked to do arts and crafts together. It was fun to create beautiful things with her. Today it was fun to shop with ideas in mind. Miss Wylie bought many crafts that we could use. That morning went by so quickly.

After shopping, she asked if I'd like to go to lunch with her. For sure, I said, "Yes!" Miss Wylie was always so nice and thoughtful of me. She treated me like family. That meant a lot because many times it was rough for me at home. My mom and dad had their problems. Alcohol had a strong hold on them and I had many sad moments because of this.

Miss Wylie knew how much I loved Mexican food so she decided to take me to a very nice place called "Panchos" in Dallas not far from my home. We were going to have a most delicious lunch for sure. It was just going to be a relaxing meal with her and me. We got into the restaurant and the hostess took us way back to a table far from the others, one in a special room.

What a surprise was there for me! As we reached that special table, there was my mom, my friend, Sister Paulette, another friend named Joan Childers, her mom and my Aunt Jean. They were all there to celebrate my sixteenth birthday.

My mom had put her problems aside that day and put me first. She planned that surprise for me and made sure my closest friends were there. I was so touched by this act of love. I remember there were presents on that table too, and they were for me.

I remember the present Sister Paulette brought me. I think I still have it packed somewhere. It was a wicker basket that the children in her class decorated for me. I knew them and they knew me because I had gone to the school where she taught and visited and played with her students. In that basket was a little snoopy dog. In my mind I can still see it today.

The funny thing was I knew it was my birthday. I just thought everyone, even Miss Wylie forgot. I also was having such a good time shopping I didn't have time to think much about it. I didn't expect anything. This was the first surprise party I ever had and I treasure that thoughtful event as one of the nicest memories of my childhood.

"…My kindness shall not depart from you, Nor shall My covenant of peace be removed, Says the Lord, who has mercy on you"
(Isaiah 54:10)

Return to Germany

– Ellinor Nieto

For my birthday in 1955, I bought a ticket to fly to Germany. Hector came along and I got him a discount since I was at that time working for the Airlines.

We visited my mother and my grandmother in Hempstead. We rented a car and went to the border to cross over to Berlin. At the border I met an old school friend who now was working for the Communists. I even said to her, "Are you kidding? Are you really working for the Red

Army?" "Yes!" she said, "and I am very proud of it." She pointed to the red flag that was flying and said, "See that flag. That is the flag that will soon take over everything." I got so upset, I said to Hector, "Let's get out of here." My school friend was saying to Hector to go and that I needed to stay. His passport showed he was from Argentina. Mine showed I was from Germany living in the USA. She was holding on to my passport and wouldn't give it back to me. I don't know what her reason was for this. I finally told her we had to leave and just took my passport from her and away we went.

We were on the autobahn and had to drive about three-hundred kilometers to get to our destination. Along the way there are many restaurants. You can just stop and go up steps, sit on top and have a meal. We stopped at one restaurant for coffee. I needed some after that experience at the border. We then had a good lunch.

We arrived in Berlin and found a nice hotel. Our room was very high and we were able to look over the wall. We could look over into East Berlin. It looked so terrible not like the Germany I grew up in. That was the east portion I was seeing. It was dark and gray and just very sad to see. My country was cut and the division was so sad to me.

I grew up very near this wall. When the Americans and English came in during the War, they saved us. We were saved from the Russians. Where I lived and where my family lived stayed free. My girlfriend at the bridge grew up near me but her family moved to the east part of Germany. When the Russians took over, she lived there and joined their army. At the border you have to go from west to east to get to Berlin. Hempstead is in West Germany. You pass through "No Man's Land" on the highway, then the East and then Berlin. It was a dangerous trip. I still shake today when I think of it.

When we were in that hotel Hector said I was his woman from

such a sad place after what we had seen and been through. He was so scared. I was, too. Our room was nice and Berlin was safe. We went shopping in the city and went to the porcelain factory there. We were engaged and were buying nice things there for our future together.

We drove back to Hempstead from Berlin. We had to go through that border crossing again. This time they were checking our passports, looking under the rental car, checking every part of the papers for the rental car and asking so many questions especially directed to me like, "Why are you living in America? You are German." My answer was because I work for

Lufthansa German Airlines in New York. They still detained us for what reason I do not know. Two Russians with machine guns approached us. The guns were pointed at us.

On the west side of the border the Americans and British soldiers noticed what was happening to us and they got into their jeeps and crossed over to where we were. We were standing outside of our rental car. They told us to get in. They told us to move our car between their jeeps. The British jeep got in front of our little Volkswagen and the American jeep went behind us. That's how we crossed back over the border.

"Enter by the narrow gate; for wide is the gate and broad is the way that leads to destruction, and there are many who go in by it."
(Matthew 7:13)

Joyce Jones playing music for one of many weddings

Songs in My Heart

— Joyce Green Jones (Lady J)

I celebrate twenty years being cancer free! I cannot let this day pass without saying something because God is able. If someone has cancer, hear me, God did it for me, one of His many children and He is able to do it for you, too. He is no respecter of persons. I thank Him because tomorrow is my anniversary. January 7, 1993, I had surgery and the cancer was removed. After that it took almost a year to complete eight chemo and twenty-five radiation treatments. Here I am still well today... twenty years later. I wouldn't trade my life for anything in the whole wide world.

God has always been in my life. Going back even as a child, He was there. My mother use to like to read romance novels and magazines. She told me that when I was four or five years old and she was reading one of those books or magazines, I went up to her with a Bible in my hand and I put it in her lap. I said, "Mom, why don't you read from this book?"

I was just a child and didn't know what I was doing, but God did. I just did what came into my heart, but the Lord was beginning a work in my mother. God has had His hand on me all of my life and I appreciate it so very much. He has given me such a wonderful life.

My mother's favorite song "Blessed Assurance" brings back many memories. She was so faithful to take us to church all through the years. We moved to Houston when I was about six years old. Mother's sister had received the Holy Ghost and she could not wait for us to get here. As soon as we arrived in Houston, Aunt Evelyn said, "Lolie, you've got to go to church with me." That's what she called my mom whose name was Viola.

My mom listened to her and it wasn't long until she received the Holy Ghost, too. We never missed a service. We went every Tuesday and Friday night, and of course, two services on Sunday. Viola Green was so faithful in taking her children…all five of us…to church. You just can't go wrong in doing that.

My dad would go to church with us sometimes and he always made sure that we had a way to go. He was a fox hunter and would go fox hunting on Saturday nights. Of course, we were a one-car family (wasn't everybody at that point in time!), so he would make sure he got home in time to clean up the car, put the back-seat back in its place, and have it all ready for us to go to Sunday school and church.

My dad was a wonderful man and so smart. He could do anything mechanically. He also really appreciated the times we would come together to sing songs and hymns. My folks bought a piano for us; they paid $50 for it. It was a great big old piano. It took several men to get it into the house because it was so heavy.

They could only afford to give piano lessons to just one of us kids at a time, so my older sister, Fern, got to take lessons first. After some-time she said, "I don't think this is my cup of tea." And so, I said, "Yay! I get to take piano lessons." And, I did and I loved every minute. We would gather many times around that piano and sing and worship the Lord. We enjoyed those times around that piano singing our favorite songs and hymns. My dad was right there and he loved it. After we would finish a song, he'd say, "Sing another one." We'd sing again. Then Dad would say, "Another." I thank the Lord today for such great memories.

"Is anyone among you suffering? Let him pray. Is anyone cheerful? Let him sing psalms." (James 5:13)

Of Dirigibles and Garlic

– Elizabeth Marshall

I was born February 21, 1922 and when I hear some stories that are about the olden days, I want to say, "I really have a good one. It is about a dirigible and I bet many people don't even know what that is today." Let me tell you what happened September 3, 1925. Though I was very young at the time, my family probably talked about it a lot afterwards and the excitement of that event makes the dirigible still a special memory to me.

I lived with my parents, Elsie Rouser Prescott and John Thomas Prescott, my sisters Ruth, Mary, and Evelyn, my grandmother, Mary Prescott and her son Edward on the farm in Pennsylvania.

On that particular night in 1925, we got to see history over our home; the USS Shenandoah dirigible flew right over our farm house. I was about three years old at the time. Though we were already in bed, probably asleep, my mother woke us and we all went outside. It was quite a sight to see. It was so huge. We had never seen anything like that. We stood out on our front porch and when it passed, it was so close to us it looked like we could almost touch it. Yes, that dirigible was just a most wondrous thing to see.

My grandmother and my uncle, my father and my mother and we four girls would have all been there the night the dirigible passed over. That was our family at the time. There probably were many more people watching with us that night because our farm always had guests who stayed with us. We probably were as much a spectacle to the people on the dirigible as that flying airship was to us.

In our family, I was the baby. My next sister, Evelyn was four years older. I do remember my mother telling me about the jobs my older sisters had on the farm. My twelve year old sister helped my father milk the cows. There were about sixteen cows and of course, in those days they milked them by hand. My sister Ruth helped with the milking. My sister Mary, we called her Bay, was the cook. She was ten and helped my mom cook all the meals on the coal stove. She would build the fire and everything.

Many people came to visit the farm from cities far away. Of course, they would stay after their long trips. I never knew what it was like to sleep in a bed in the summer time because we had so many visitors. My sister Evelyn and I usually slept together on the floor in our parents' bedroom during that time. The guests needed our beds.

Some relatives came with three boys one summer. The boys slept in the barn. They'd just crawl into the hayloft and stay there at night. They helped with the work around the farm. One of those boys really didn't like school at all and so he stayed on the farm all the time with my parents, helping them out doing various chores and working for different neighbors. Since he was always with us, he became part of our family and was like a brother to us.

Everybody was welcomed on our farm so our family was always large. My mother baked bread often. She'd bake ten to twelve loaves most of the time. There were so many people to feed. Most everyone worked hard when they came to visit us. My father and mother worked hard and so did my sisters. Evelyn probably helped take care of me. I was the only one who didn't have to do much of anything. I just had to play. I had the easiest job. When I was older I never had to milk the cows. I did learn to take them out to pasture and bring them back. I'd put them out to pasture in the morning and bring them back in the afternoon. Once in a while one would be contrary and wouldn't want to come back but it would give up and finally follow me with the rest of the herd.

I remember once sitting out in the garden eating garlic when I was quite little. I must have liked it. My older sisters would get so angry because their boyfriends would come and I would be on those boys' knees smelling like garlic. I suppose that garlic helped me stay healthy and keep a great memory.

I've often thought that the way we lived, even the fact that as a child I usually ran and seldom walked has added to my long life. Maybe the secret to all my years is garlic and great exercise like running. And then again, maybe my sisters made me run because of the garlic. I don't know but I am grateful for my many years and the great memories that fill them.

"But those who wait on the Lord shall renew their strength… They shall run and not be weary."
(Isaiah 40:31)

Ready to Help

—Sanny Laxton

I lived next door to my parents when my dad got very sick. My mother called me and said, "Daddy fell in the back yard and he can't get up." I went over and I couldn't pick him up. He was six-feet tall and a big man. I pulled and pushed until I got him into the house and up on his bed. My brother came over and helped me and then we took him to the hospital. He stayed a week in the hospital and then they released him and sent him back home.

Back home my dad still was very weak and couldn't take care of himself. My mother needed help with him. I started taking care of him. I changed diapers and washed him. He was embarrassed and I was, too. He was my dad. I finally said, "Dad, look I am now your nurse, not your daughter." This helped him; it broke the embarrassment.

After a week I noticed my dad was getting no better. I called my brother and he came and took Daddy to the doctor. Even with the doctor visits and the medicine, Daddy continued to be weak and fall often. My mother couldn't help him because she was in the first stages of Alzheimer's. I was glad God gave me strength and opportunity to take care of both of them. And, that is what I did.

Since Daddy continued to fall a lot, we decided to try a different doctor. This doctor told us that Daddy had what some babies had when the top of their head at birth didn't grow together. No one knew how long he had lived with that condition. The doctor explained that possibly it was the cause of him falling down so much. He said the fluid from the spine would build up and press on Daddy's brain. He said that my dad needed a very dangerous operation to correct this problem.

The doctor told us that Daddy only had a twenty per-cent survival chance with the operation that he needed. I went to the chapel and was praying for my dad. I felt the Spirit tell me right then and there that my dad would be well and he would walk again.

Daddy came out of surgery and did recover. He had weeks of therapy. The physical therapist taught me how to do the therapy with him at home. We continued that therapy three times a day and slowly Daddy improved. One day I was walking behind him and noticed he was picking up his walker while he was walking. He was really carrying it, not using it to help him walk.

My brother came by and noticed the same thing. My dad didn't even realize he was walking on his own. Daddy finally realized what he was doing and put that walker away. God promised a miracle and gave it to my dad. He lived and walked without a walker for nine more years.

My family appreciated my care for my daddy. When he went to Heaven, I would check on Mom who was then in a nursing home. My family recognized my willingness and ability to help; relatives would ask me to care for family members in need. I would visit nursing homes where relatives lived and help others in their homes. I would cook and care for them and through the years I was always ready to help my family as their "family nurse on call."

"If you have faith as a mustard seed you will say to this mountain, move from here to there, and it will move; and nothing will be impossible for you." (Matthew 17:20)

Ophelia with husband and three of her babies

Value of Hard Work

– Ophelia Deanda

P eople say to me, "Tell me the secret of why you are still moving around, doing so much, looking so young. It is hard to believe you are eighty-six." I tell them it is because I worked hard when I was young. I remember always working hard. That is just how it was when I was growing up.

The earliest memory I have of my childhood is when I was about twelve or thirteen years old. We would walk to school about a mile or two and then catch the bus. My mother would make our lunch. We were poor and Mom couldn't buy bread. She would make biscuits and put beans seasoned with chili powder. They were delicious to us.

Most of the other kids brought lunches with fruit and cookies. I don't remember feeling liked by most of those kids. There was one girl, though, who was really nice to me. She was my friend and sometimes she would even share a half of her apple or some other fruit with me. I stayed in school until sixth grade. Then, my brother and I started working in the fields picking cotton with my dad on a farm in west Texas.

Sometimes when my dad would be on the tractor and the two of us, my brother and I were picking cotton, he'd stop and say he was going home to get something to eat.

He'd tell us, "You two keep picking cotton. I'll bring you back lunch." As soon as he'd leave, we'd pick that little brown part off before the cotton ball opens and we'd throw those at each other. My brother was about ten years old then and I was fourteen. Dad never knew what we did so we never got in trouble for it.

My mother used to wash our clothes outside in a bucket. My brother and I would go to a place in the camp where we lived and get the water for her. They had the water in a big old tank. We'd fill our bucket with that water. Mother would fix a fire under the bucket of water for the clothes to get it hot. Those clothes would come out so very nice that our neighbors would ask how she got them so clean. We'd help her hang them outside on a line to dry.

I worked also cleaning a lady's house. She had a very nice house. I would have to get on the floor with a rag and really scrub all along the corners and the floors. It was hard work, but I didn't mind. I don't remember how much I got paid, but I learned many different ways to clean and like I said, I really worked hard.

Sometimes I even helped kill the chickens they would cook. Someone would hang that chicken on a wire outside and then I would be given the knife to cut off its head. I did it because it was my job. Then the lady would put that chicken in hot water and I'd pluck out the feathers. I wouldn't want to do that job today, but then I didn't mind.

When I was older I did a very different job. I worked in a factory that packed eggs to send overseas. I had to separate the whites from the yolks in each egg. I would crack the egg, separate the eggs putting the whites in one can and the yolks in another. There was a machine there with a light in it. I'd put the egg in that machine and if the yolk was directly in the middle, that egg would be put in the first class section. The eggs that had yolks not directly in the middle would just be classified as ordinary eggs. I guess people would pay more for the first class ones.

They would mark them with an "A" or a double "AA." This job was not so hard but it was long and tiring.

When I was twenty-two, I met my husband. We fell in love, married and had nine children, four boys and five girls. I continued to work during these years. Now, my hard work was at home for my husband and for my children.

"Therefore…he will be a vessel for honor, sanctified and useful for the Master, prepared for every good work." (2 Timothy 2:21)

I Care

— Ellinor Nieto

My feet started itching again and I moved to New York and got a job in the Booth Memorial Hospital in Flushing. The hospital was run by the Salvation Army. I was a nurse's aide here for the preemies. They trained me in two days teaching me how to make the formula and sterilize the water for these little babies. Sometimes I had twenty-eight babies to take care of and feed. They were so little.

One of these little babies weighed less than four lbs. and they told me that he was going to be my baby to take care of specially. So I did and I named him Charlie. I would say, "Charlie, come on. This is not your mama. This is your nanny. You be nice and eat this good formula. I made it just for you." He would just suck so fast and drink that whole bottle. I would give him a little water. He would just suck away. I would say, "Charlie, you are not the prettiest baby here in the nursery but I love you." He would just grin up at me. I will never forget that grin. It was just so precious.

I had rented a room in an apartment building near the hospital. The landlady was nice to me. She let me have the run of the house and even work in the garden. She trusted me so much. One day she said, "I am going to be away for approximately six weeks. I am going to Miami and you're going to be in charge of the whole house. Here are the keys for everything." I was so stunned and I said to her, "You trust me so much." She said, "I've watched you and I trust you even with everything." I was crying when she said that.

At the hospital I got friendly with an Irish girl named Sally. She was so pretty with her brown hair and rosy cheeks. She said to me one day, "You never go out." Oh, oh, I knew she was talking about dating.

I kept telling her no I wasn't interested. Finally she persuaded me to go on a double date with her. I got all dressed up and my landlady said she would answer the door and check my date out for me. She said she would check him out before he came into the house.

The doorbell rang. She went to answer it. She said, "Just one second, please." She came to me and said, "He looks okay. I guess you can go out to dinner on a double date. Take my telephone number and if something goes funny there, just call me. I'll call the police." She really was my guardian angel. She was like my second mother.

The door was open and she said, "You should see his car. It looks brand new. A red MG sports car." I asked if the hood was down. She said yes and I should take a scarf for my hair. I got the scarf and went out to meet my date. He was very polite as he opened my door for me and introduced himself saying, "Hello, I'm Hector." I'm pleased to meet you."

"Whoever receives one of these little children in My name receives Me; and whoever receives Me, receives not Me, but Him who sent Me." (Mark 9:37)

Strength in Weakness

– Dorothy Wiggins

When your loved one has a need, you will do anything you can to help out. I think about this when I remember how sick my brother was when he was seven years old. He had polio. He was in a hospital in Houston, Texas in an iron lung. I don't remember what year it was but it was during that first epidemic of polio in the United States. Not a lot was known about this disease and many children were getting it. The kind of polio my brother had was the most serious kind. He was paralyzed and in a coma.

They did a tracheotomy so he could have a tube to help him breathe and they put him in an iron lung. If you've never seen an iron lung, let me tell you, they're gruesome things to see. They are big cylinder things that the person is put into and this machine actually makes the person breathe with its compressions and depressions.

My dad happened to be at the hospital one day when there was a terrible thunder storm in the area. That iron lung was electric and the electricity went off. At the back of the iron lung was a hand pump. You could pump the machine manually but it was hard to do. My brother would have died without that pump working and the hospital was short-handed during that storm. Everybody who had any strength at all was asked to please help with the pump and they were all instructed to pump it as you breathe yourself. To pump too quickly would not have been safe.

My dad went to the foot of my brother's iron lung and he pumped and he pumped. He was terrified. He was praying, "God, give me strength to do this." He wasn't use to this. It was heavy manual labor for him. He was really struggling to keep his son alive. He was almost to the point of exhaustion. But, he wouldn't give up.

Someone said to him, "Brother Ford." He looked up and there was Brother Henry Rose, a friend of his. He said, "The Lord sent me." My dad said, "I can't turn loose." Brother Rose said, "Yes, you can. The Lord sent me. And, I'm going to do this in your place." He had to pry my daddy's hands off that pump because he was pumping for his son with all his might. At last he let go and Brother Rose took over. He became God's extended arm to my dad and my brother. God didn't forget my brother or my dad in this time of trouble. God is awesome! When you need Him, He is always there.

"Trust in the Lord forever, for in…
the Lord is everlasting strength."
(Isaiah 26:4)

Mother Lucille comes to church with Joyce and Harry.

God Honors Prayer

—Joyce Wiggins

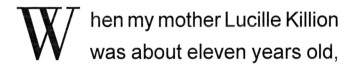

hen my mother Lucille Killion
was about eleven years old,

a lady came to her home to visit. Her home was way out in the country and had no modern conveniences. Her mother and father didn't even have a car. They had eight children, the youngest being Lucille. And they very seldom had visitors. So, this visit was very special. The lady came to witness about God. Lucille and her brothers and sisters joined their parents as they listened to this lady.

After the lady left, little Lucille went way back in the field behind her house. She looked up to Heaven and said, "God, I would like to be saved, but I don't know how. I don't even know what to say." Thank God, He answered a little girl's sincere prayer.

Lucille grew in that home in the country and when she was sixteen she married her twenty-one year old beau, Ben Rapsilver. Both Ben and Lucille had accepted the Lord and were baptized before I was born. In fact, I was in my mother while she was being baptized.

My brothers Benny and Tommy and I knew Jesus right away. We were blessed by the example of Mother and Father, who from the beginning made sure our home was a Christian one. When God chose Lucille and Ben Rapsilver for each other, they chose Him as their Savior and our parents weren't going to let us be left out. The prayer the little eleven year old girl made so many years ago continued and God honored her faith even through her children.

After my father passed away, my mother continued her witness to and for the Lord to her children, grand-children, great-grand-children and everyone she met. She remained always strong in her faith and in the Lord. Even her physical health remained strong to the very end. At ninety years old, Mother started to weaken physically and couldn't stay home alone. My niece Rebecca came and lived with her. Rebecca was a great comfort because Mother could continue to stay at home close to family and friends.

When my precious mother took a turn for the worse during that last month, I went to be with her every day. As she lay on her bed in her home, we watched her slowly slip away. The Lord honored her prayer those many years ago and on February 1, 2005, He came to take her Home with Him. We all stood by her bed, her children, grand-children, great-grand-children and all of our extended family. We took turns singing to her the old hymns she loved.

We didn't know if she heard us. We just hoped that she did. I was so tired I would sit on the couch, lean my head back and pray. I said, "Lord, we are now ready to let her go."

He said to me, "This time was not for her, but for all of you." I told the family. I understood in my heart that God gave us this time to remember Mother and her life. She lived for God and was a Christian example to all of us. Jesus gave us this time to tell her good-bye.

"Yea, though I walk through the valley of the shadow of death, I will fear no evil; For You are with me…"
(Psalm 23:4)

Finding a Place

—Ellinor Nieto

One day a lady came. She said, "I have been looking all over for you. I know a family who needs someone to care for their children. I told them about you and they want you." I said, "No way!" My friend assured me saying, "The father is a hotel manager in Miami Beach and he and his wife want you. They will even pay for your plane ticket. They really want you to be the one to care for their children. Can I tell them you are interested?" I said, "Go call them right now and tell them I am more that interested. I am on the next plane out." Before I knew it, I was on my way to Miami.

When I departed from my plane in Miami, my new boss met me at the airport. He was tall and good looking and drove me to the hotel in his light green Cadillac. He showed me my quarters and told me to take my time since they had already hired a baby sitter for that day. They invited me to learn my way around and even use the swimming pool. So on this first day I did relax and even swam in that nice pool.

There were cabanas on the side of the pool. I learned that older ladies and men would sit there and play cards, a game called "Battle." I would often sit there with the baby and enjoy watching them in that game. Sometimes they would want me to go for a swim and offer to watch the baby. They would want me to play cards with them, too. I just wouldn't though because that baby was my responsibility. I didn't want anything to happen to her. They were so nice to me though and I appreciated it. One of the men even gave me a book of a stamp collection. It was very beautiful and I kept it for years.

In the city of Miami I had a different experience. One day I went on the bus just to go shopping and when I got on the bus I went and sat in the back of the bus. The bus driver stopped the bus and came to me. He said, "You need to come with me and sit here." I asked him, "Why?" He then brought me to the very front and told me that the back of the bus was for the black people. He said that I could not sit there. That was in 1955. This was a sad surprise to me. I had never heard of such a thing before. I asked him again, "Why?" He said that it was the rule and we just had to follow it.

My boss was worried because I wasn't going out on dates. He wanted to get me a "blind date." I said, "No! No! No blind dates for me." He said,

"No he is really nice. His name is Seymour." He was working at the hotel. He said Seymour would take me out to a nice place. I finally said alright and went and got all dressed up for my date.

Seymour came in a pair trousers and a polo shirt and he said he didn't know where to take me. He said his boss just got him into this. He didn't seem to really want it and for sure I didn't either. He asked me where I wanted to go. I didn't know any place. He didn't either and ended up taking me to a place around the corner. We walked there from the hotel. It was very noisy and only guys were there. I was the only girl and everyone looked at me. It was a hangout where I didn't belong. I didn't even sit at a table in there. I just made a U-turn and we left. I think after that Seymour needed to change his name to "See nothing."

"Many are the afflictions of the righteous, But the Lord delivers him out of them all." (Psalm 34:19)

An Anointing

— Sanny Laxton

My son was a Marine stationed in Guam. He was on different six month tours in that area. He wrote me and said he would be going for his next assignment/tour in the Persian Gulf between Iran and Iraq.

One day I had a vision of a ship that was docked in Singapore and another vision of another ship having a religious service on board. I heard the Holy Spirit say within me. "Your son's ship was docked in Singapore to be re-fueled and while they were docked there, they received orders to go to Somalia." I started getting scared because I had heard of the uprisings they were having there in Somalia.

I had been praying for Somalia because I had heard of their suffering. People were starving there and there was so much cruelty going on. I really feared for my son. I was standing there thinking of him. Suddenly I felt like oil was being poured over me, over my head and all the way down to the floor. Immediately I felt such peace. No more fear. I felt God had poured the oil of peace all over me.

Sometime later, I was watching TV. It was early morning in Somalia and the reporters were showing the Marines coming ashore there. They had spotlights on the Marines as they were coming off the ship. I got angry. I felt if I would have been there I would have wanted to shoot those reporters. It seemed to me those pictures on the television were putting our brave military in danger.

Later there was a program showing the Marines at the airport. They were setting up their camp at the hangar. I saw my son during that program. I was surprised and I went over to see my family that night and told them I had seen Ronnie on TV. They said they had seen him, too. We were thinking he was in the Persian Gulf. And here he was in Somalia.

Two weeks later I got a letter from Ronnie, saying when they had stopped in Singapore their orders were changed from the Persian Gulf to Somalia. He told me that he went on patrol and they had to dig fox holes. They could only dig about two feet deep. They would keep hitting rock. He told me he remembered something he learned from me when he helped back home in our garden. There was a rock hoe in their truck, like the one Grandma, my mother used. She would walk around the yard with that hoe and dig all the rocks out so we could plant our garden. When the Marines hit rock, he just got that hoe and went to work, taking out those rocks making the fox hole deeper and safer. His friends knew he was kin to Grandma after that. He remembered what he learned back home and it paid off for him and his Marine buddies way over in Somalia.

After Somalia, my son went to Iraq and later to Afghanistan. I prayed for him, his troops and the allies that were there with him. This time God didn't send His Spirit with that oil of peace. He left me on my own. I knew Ronnie would be safe though and he was. God must have trusted me to not worry and more. Now, my son is back home and retired from service. I can relax a little more and know the only time he'll be using a hoe is in his garden.

"Behold, how good and how pleasant it is For brethren to dwell together in unity! It is like the precious oil upon the head, Running down..." (Psalm 133:1, 2)

Two fishermen on vacation

Nosey Questions

—Joyce Wiggins

S everal years ago they would ask nosey questions when you

went to get your fishing license. We were in a line to get our license. Many people were in front of us and more people behind us. When it was our turn, I told my husband Harry to go first and he did. Then he stepped aside and I moved up in line.

The man started asking the usual questions like name and address. I showed him my driver's license. Then he asked my age. I answered quickly and he said, "Wow! Most women hesitate at that question." I said, "We're probably going to have problems with one of the other questions." I knew which one. I had heard what he had asked Harry.

He tried to find out what the hard question would be and said, "Which one is that?" I just told him to go on with his questions. He said, "Okay! How much do you weigh?" I said, "That's it." He said it again, "How much do you weigh?" I backed up and twirled around and said, "Guess!" He said, "You've got to be kidding." I said, "Nope. Guess!"

The poor man looked at the long line waiting and he said, "Okay!" Then, he wrote down a number and showed it to me. He had knocked off fifteen pounds. So, I gave him a thumb's up and said, "That will work." As we walked away, Harry said, "You really embarrass me." I said, "Well, sometimes you just have to do what you've got to do!"

"To everything there is a season…a time to laugh…a time to keep silence, and a time to speak."
(Ecclesiastes 3:1, 4, 7)

No Regular Party

—Mary Rose Falgoust

My stepdad was very special to me. I called him "Paw-Paw" and he was to me a real dad. When my mom had to be placed in a nursing home, he went every day to visit her and be with her. When she died, my husband and I invited him to stay with us for a few days. He was glad and said his house was too lonely. He came for those few days and ended up staying for ten years.

When he was ninety-eight, we saw him becoming very weak. Even though we made sure he was never alone, he would often fall. When I would have to be away from the house for my meetings, my husband would always watch out for him. We both loved him very much and didn't want anything to happen to him. He had told us of his wish for his hundredth birthday. He said, "I don't want just a regular party. I want a real live band and lots of people." We never forgot these words. I don't think he would let us.

As time passed, he became weaker and fell often. We realized that my job would at times call us away from home and knew we could never leave Paw-Paw home alone. We knew that even with us there, he was falling and getting hurt. The week before Easter, I took him to the doctor to see what the doctor would recommend. I'll never forget that visit. After examining Paw-Paw, the doctor told me, "It's time." My heart was broken. I cried because that meant I needed to place this sweet gentle man who had become my dad into a nursing home. He was too much at risk to be at home with my husband and me. The doctor told me that this was the only option for us. We could no longer take care of Paw-Paw and we knew it. He needed round the clock nursing care.

We found the best place and it was near our home. It was Good Friday, a couple of days after that doctor's visit when we took him to his new home, the nursing home. He was there for about a year and a half. We would visit Paw-Paw every day and knew he was safe and well cared for. In our visits we often reminded him of the promise we made about his one-hundredth birthday. We kept track of that coming date, telling him each time with words like, "It's getting closer Paw-Paw. It's getting closer." I promised him the greatest party ever, with a band and with so many people just like he wanted. We were going to keep our promise to him. I would say, "Only six more months," and he would give me that smile.

About a month before his hundredth birthday, we told him

everything was ready. We had gotten him a band and sent out many invitations. Finally the day arrived, Paw-Paw's one-hundredth birthday. His two real daughters (daughters he had never gotten to know), his brother, so many family members and friends from all over came to celebrate with him. They all came for him and so did his real live band. We kept our promise and Paw-Paw knew it and loved every minute. His party was wonderful and he got so much love and attention from everyone. The whole nursing home enjoyed that music and Paw-Paw, though he couldn't dance in his wheel chair, jiggled his feet with every beat. He loved that music and he loved his one-hundredth birthday celebration on this June 16th. We realized how he hung on for this promise kept. On July 18th, one month and two days later, Paw-Paw passed away quietly to celebrate with a Heavenly band in a dance that lasts forever, no wheel chair needed.

"Then David danced before the Lord with all his might..." (2 Samuel 6:14)

Nurse's Aide in England

– Ellinor Nieto

After a short vacation in Germany telling my family and friends good-bye, I booked my passage to England. I was going to start in a new position as a nurse's aide in a sanatorium for heart patients. It was situated in a lovely surrounding with such a beautiful landscape. The people were very friendly to me even though it was shortly after WWII. I wasn't sure how I would be treated being as I was from Germany. Everyone was very kind.

On my days off I would take the train into London for shopping. It was great and the prices were even greater. I stayed in England for approximately two and a half years. At the end of those years I worked for the matron in charge of the whole place. Her husband was in the German Army and she had been in the English Army. She still walked like she was in the army and everybody was afraid of her. They would always say, "Please, go ask her something for me." They were too frightened. I would tell them to go ask her themselves but they would respond that they were too afraid of her. She was always nice to me. I certainly was not afraid of her at all. I loved her and she did like me.

Julie was the matron's dog and I took care of her Julie. When her maid let Julie loose one day Julie got too friendly with Ben, the farmer's dog, and sometime later, about nine weeks, Julie had five little puppies. Julie became a mama with quite a mixture. Three looked just like mama, little black Cocker Spaniels and two looked like tiny Golden Retrievers, imitations of Ben, the farmer's dog.

Though she looked tough, this big woman could not even handle these little puppies. One of them died and she just couldn't bring herself to take care of it. I buried that little thing for her in the yard. She took a picture once of me kneeling at the bottom of the steps holding one and trying to get another in my arms.

When the puppies were old enough, the matron gave them away to friends. One she gave to her niece; that was a memorable experience. Her niece is Patricia Kirkland a very famous and beautiful English movie star. While I was at the matron's bungalow, I got to meet this star in person. I still remember how beautiful she was with her long black hair. I had so many nice experiences during my years in England I still remember them fondly. After

England I had my heart on a new job in a new country. Soon I would leave England for America.

"Therefore you shall deal kindly with your servant, for you have brought your servant into a covenant of the Lord with you."
(1 Samuel 20:8)

Havert and Darlene Witte celebrating
their 50th Wedding Anniversary

Finding the Most Beautiful

— Havert Witte with help
from daughter Verna

I am ninety-one years old and let
me tell you what I remember. I

was born and raised in this country. The day I was born was January 4, 1922. I remember my dad breaking up the land to make a garden. He had a mule and a pair of oxen to help him plow our land. He planted many flowers and other garden plants. We had vegetables in our garden, peach trees, watermelon and so many good things to eat. I would say our garden was beautiful.

There were two girls whose mother had died when the girls were very young. Their aunt took care of them. They lived about four miles from my home. One night the two girls and I went out together to a dance. When it was time to get in the car, Darlene got into the car and sat next to me and after that we just kept going together getting closer and closer.

Though Darlene was just sixteen and I was twenty-seven, our ages did not matter. We were in love and so we did the right thing. We became Mr. and Mrs. Havert Witte. What a wonderful day that was, May 12, 1949. From that day, we worked hard together making our own home and then raising our two little girls Linda and Verna. I would see beauty everywhere but the most beautiful was always my sweet Darlene.

When my girls were small I was working downtown in Houston, Texas. One of the guys at work took me aside and asked me many questions. He liked my way of doing what I did and liked my answers to his questions, too. I was good at my job and after he asked me all of those questions, he hired me as a supervisor. I needed to work night shifts to break a new boy in on the job. Since I worked at night I would try to sleep for a time during the day.

My little girl Linda was full of fire more so than you can imagine. She would get herself into trouble easily. One day, I was sound asleep, taking a nap. That is what I did when I worked at night. All of a sudden my wife ran into the bedroom and said, "Come on, Hon! Linda needs you!" I ran into the kitchen and there she was with her little head caught behind the stove and she just couldn't get out. I said, "That won't be bad. She's not hurt is she?" And, sure enough she wasn't hurt, just scared and stuck. I told my wife, "It's a good thing you didn't move that stove." It would have blown up. I carefully reached back and told my little girl not to touch anything because the stove was hot. She listened and I got her out. I was so glad. We would have died had anything bad happened to her. She was so scared and so were we.

After that, every time I would go anywhere, my little girl would want to go with me. If I went squirrel hunting she would want to go. If I was just walking around the house, she would grab my hand and walk with me. She was her daddy's little girl. She was both the wildest and the best little girl ever. She really kept me busy and my wife, too.

Both of my girls grew up and did well in grade school and high school. Boys would come around and I would check them out. My wife, Darlene and I worked hard. We wanted Linda and Verna to have the best. They both graduated from high school with honors. We helped and supported them in finding work and getting them transportation. They always made us so very proud of them.

Linda was the first to marry. She met and fell in love with a son of one of my hunting buddies. Verna married Ralph, a boy she met in high school. Darlene saw him first and had already picked him out for our youngest daughter because he was so handsome and she wanted her little girl to have the best.

My two daughters, Linda and Verna had both found the loves of their lives and gave us four beautiful grand-children and three great-grand-children. We were happy for them and prayed that they would have beautiful lives like Darlene and I.

I have a hard time remembering things but I remember my beautiful wife, Darlene and my two beautiful little girls all grown up and this makes me feel good.

"Let your adornment be…the hidden person of the heart, with the incorruptible beauty of a gentle and quiet spirit which is very precious in the sight of God." (1 Peter 3:3-4)

Heavenly Push

– Sarah Duplease

This happened when I was still in the mind of God. I hadn't been born yet. My mother told me this story often. It happened around 1934.

My family lived in Pueblo, Colorado. Dad owned a gas station. They needed to travel through many hills and valleys as they went from town to town to shop or to take care of other needs. There were no bridges in the area. The hills were high and the valleys very low. Flash floods in the area were dangerous. At one time, a dam broke and the water flooded a whole town.

One day my father and mother, George and Ana Duplease, my two older sisters and my brother were traveling from one town to another in Colorado. There was a heavy down-pour. My dad was driving his black Packard with those big lights that look like bulging eyes. I don't know where they were going but the whole family was in that car.

The rain started pouring down suddenly in torrents. There had been times before when heavy rains caused flash flooding. My parents had three very small children in the car, a reason to be more concerned. George was only two. Mary was four and Sally was six. Both of my parents knew at that moment they were in danger on the road. My dad was driving carefully to avoid any mishap as he neared the top of a hill. All was fine until the car reached the bottom. There in the deepest part, it stalled. Dad tried to restart that car and the engine just wouldn't turn on.

My mother looked through the rear view window and saw a huge gush of water rushing down the hill towards them. She and my dad began praying as Dad continued trying to start the car. It just wouldn't do anything. The water was getting closer. I can't imagine what my mom thought as she looked at Dad and my brother and sisters.

Suddenly, that Packard's motor turned on and that old car climbed up the hill with Dad, Mom, my brother and two sisters. As they reached the top, they could see that the water had rushed down and covered the spot right where they had just been. Mom and Dad knew what God had just done for them.

Ana and George never doubted that angels came that rainy day when a real heavenly push was needed. They recalled the story of the rescue from the rushing waters, the day the old Packard needed a heavenly push and got it, the day

God sent His angels to their rescue. Their children present and those still to come, like me, heard this most important part of our family history all through the years as were growing up.

"He shall give His angels charge over you. In their hands they shall bear you up." (Matthew 4:6)

Mud Pies to Clouds Gone by

−Lois Horton

I was the baby in my family. My older sister was fifteen years older so I don't remember playing much with her. I do remember having fun with many cousins who lived near us. We would get together and make mud pies in the yard and then have a party and pretend to eat them. One of my cousins came by with a grasshopper I caught. He killed it and then was really going to eat it. I remember that. He almost did eat it. I don't know how we got him to not do such a thing. That is a memory to have. It is just the first one that comes to me. It would have been so disgusting if my cousin would have eaten that bug.

When I was much older I was a nurse. I went to school and got my Masters in psychology. I became in charge of an assertiveness class. This was my pride and joy. It definitely was one of my treasured accomplishments. I had the privilege of being in charge of this program for years in a state hospital. I used the theory of Eric Burns, *I'm Okay. You're Okay.* My patients became so free through these classes. Many learned to be and find friends.

Literally I saw clouds lift from their lives. So many were living in shells and were so unhappy. They didn't know how to express themselves and found themselves always down. They were like people run over and couldn't say what they really needed to. They were lost in depression.

It was really such a joy for me to see the changes in people who had lived years without much hope. Through openness and sharing, many walls came down and some saw sunshine in their lives where only storms existed before. I was very grateful to be a part of this in so many lives.

After the course, many continued through out-patient counseling and though it took longer, changes came and more clouds disappeared. Some of course needed medication to help but it always touched me deeply when I could see the many changes that came about just because persons learned to communicate and appreciate who and why they were.

"Your testimonies are wonderful; Therefore my soul keeps them."
(Psalm 119:129)

Mama Betty with children, Ceaylon, Betty Jean, Dimple, Irene and Dwight

In His Presence

– Dimple Odom

My brothers and sisters were all working when Mama got too ill to care for herself. My sister Betty Jean had almost died that year in 1986, too. There was no one who could stay with Mama all the time and she needed round the clock care. There was a nursing home that I would pass every day on my way to work so we thought of possibly placing Mama there for a while. When we realized this was not the best for her, we made other plans.

Mama had worked so very hard and she was very frugal. She had saved her money well. She had property in Louisiana that we sold for her, too. We decided that it would be right to spend every penny needed to get her the best care. So, she went back home with my brother Dwight to Pasadena, Texas and we hired someone to stay with her during the day. Dwight and Mickey were there at night. On my days off from the hospital I would go and be with her during the day. One of us was always there to care for her.

After some time she started having little mini strokes, TIA's they called them. She lost some ground with that, and the little activity she could manage made it worse. After Mom's seventy-sixth birthday on August 11, 1987, her health began to quickly deteriorate. We never left her. Even my brother Ceaylon from Louisiana came over on weekends and stayed with Mama when he was able. Because she had liver damage, she went into a hepatic coma. The strangest thing was that Mama stayed so alert. My oldest sister Irene from Louisiana came to see her. It was like she and Mama had some closure they had to make before Mama could rest.

After Irene's visit, my darling Mama was ready. She just slipped into a coma. She said to me, "Dimple, I am passing the torch to you." I felt that she meant the burden she had for my brothers and sisters, she wanted me to take to heart for the Lord. She didn't want any of her children to be lost. I took off work, telling my supervisor that I would stay with my mother now until it was her time to leave us, no matter how many days it would be.

Mama had told us she didn't want to go back to the hospital. She just wanted to be with us at home. So, we honored her wishes. All we wanted to do for her now was to keep her comfortable. The doctor gave me medicine to give her to keep her out of pain. For about five days I felt she didn't want to leave us. Even though she couldn't talk, it was like her spirit and my spirit were united. I could feel her communicating with me. One night while my brothers were in with her, I stepped in and said, "Mama, you need to let us go because we are ready to let you go."

On September 29, 1987 I was in the bathroom getting ready for the day, my sister-in-law, Toy, came in and said, "Dimple, you need to come. Mama has opened her eyes." I went in and yes, her eyes were opened and fixed toward the foot of her bed. She looked so alert. I knew she was dying though, because I had seen many people die before. I also knew Mama was seeing something, something only her eyes could behold. We could see nothing.

In that room God's Presence was so strong, we could feel it. My nephew was at Mama's side reading one of her favorite passages from Isaiah about mounting up with wings as eagles, running and not growing weary. We were crying and praising God at the same time. As the Lord came and took my mother away, it was the most glorious moment I've ever experienced.

I have stood at the bedside of many people who have died and never ever felt as I did that time in my mother's room. We all knew it was God's affirmation to us in our sadness, giving us peace. We were losing our mother now but, He was taking her Home with Him forever. He let us be present and witness that glorious moment. I have never forgotten it and neither will my brothers, sisters and nephew. I don't believe any of us ever could.

"But they that wait upon the Lord Shall renew their strength; They shall mount up with wings as eagles; They shall run, and not be weary; They shall walk, and not faint." (Isaiah 40:31)

Bermuda

– Ellinor Nieto

We stayed in Hamilton Bermuda at a cottage of Matthias, who was a friend of Hector. We arrived very early, too early for Matthias. We arrived around 5:00 a.m. and couldn't get in. We sat out in the garden. I was very hungry and tired.

There were salamanders all over in that garden. They were crawling all over the flowers and benches, etc. They would stop and look at me with those big eyes. It came to a point where I began talking to one of the salamanders. I said, "Do you have any food for me? I'm hungry." They would just look at me and then run away.

Matthias finally arrived with the keys for our cottage. It was in such a beautiful location with flowers all around. We went into the cottage and I decided to take a shower right away. We had been traveling for over twenty-four hours and I needed a shower. I took one first. I was in the shower singing. The hot water was just running over my body and my hair. It felt so wonderful. I was so happy to have that shower.

I came out and Hector decided to take a long hot shower, too. He got in and started to shower and the next thing I heard was screaming. It was Hector and he was saying really bad things in Spanish. Then he began in English, "This woman took all my hot water! Now, I am here standing in ice cold water." He came out of the shower and he said, "You woman, you took all my hot water. What am I going to do now?"

I suggested that Hector take a swim in the pool since there was no more hot water. So, I got him over being so angry. Finally I was standing dressed already to go to have lunch. He decided to go back and take an ice cold shower. He was still saying,

"Woman, woman, woman" while he was in that shower.

We went across the street to the Elbow Beach Restaurant and had the most delicious lunch. We had lobster, scampi, salad and delicious home-made bread. We kept asking for more of that bread to dip into the dressing. It was so absolutely delicious.

After lunch we got into our bathing suits and went down to the beach. The ocean was as clear as glass. We could see little fish swimming around our feet. I was saying, "Hey, don't you bite me!" to those fish. Hector and I walked on the beach later. It was so delightful. At night, a nice breeze blew right through the curtains in our cottage. It was so quiet, peaceful and cool. Everything was unbelievable. I closed my eyes and said with a smile, "Good night Bermuda!"

"For you shall go out with joy, And be led out with peace; The mountains and the hills Shall break forth into singing before you, And all the trees of the field shall clap their hands." (Isaiah 55:12)

Being There for Each Other

—Josephine Matthey

There were seven children in our family, three girls and four boys. I was the third oldest. I remember when my older brother and I were in elementary school. My family lived in San Antonio on a street in back of St. Henry's School. We both went to Briscoe Elementary together and every day we would walk home for lunch.

I can still see my mother standing on the front porch looking so ready for us with her clean apron and her hair fixed so nicely. Every day there she would be waiting for us, making sure we were safe as we walked home. She had our lunch ready and we'd eat together. Then she'd go back to the porch with us and watch as we walked back to school. My brother was older. I was about thirteen years old.

Another thing I remember about my mom is she didn't work away from home. She did everything at home, making sure the house was always clean, that all of us took care of ourselves and each other and she cooked all our meals. She did everything around the house. She was there all the time.

My father worked at two jobs while I was growing up. His first job was with a packing company and he sold meat for them. He would go to different towns to get meat orders during the day and later in the after-noon he was a butcher at Highland's Butcher Shop.

Among my memories is one especially sad one. When I was in junior high, my oldest sister died of Rheumatic Fever. It was hard on all of us and very hard on my mother. I remember my sister being sick in the bedroom in the front of our house. I would see my mother putting towels on her. I didn't know what was wrong with her. When she passed away, they had her body put in the living room with those candles on the side of her. I cried because I didn't understand. I really thought she would get up and she didn't. I was young and didn't know any better.

My sister's death was even sadder because she was engaged to be married. Her fiancé was in the army and I remember him coming for the funeral. The church where the funeral was going to be was St. Henry's and it was three blocks away. We walked to the church from our house. Her fiancé walked in front of the hearse. It was so very sad.

Another memory that comes to me was my own engagement. I had taken cosmetology in high school and after I graduated, I became a hairdresser. I didn't work very long because soon after graduation Julius Matthey Sr. and I became engaged. In those days young men were drafted and right after we married, my new husband was drafted. I went to live with my mother-in-law, father-in-law and Julius's grandmother.

After basic training, my husband was stationed in Fort Knox, Kentucky. My father-in-law bought Julius a used car and helped me get to Fort Knox to be with him. My in-laws were always so kind to us.

While in Fort Knox, Julius and I had our first baby. Our family lived there on the base in a little duplex. One night while we were eating supper, a blue car drove up with the chaplain, my husband's sergeant, and another person. They came to tell us that Julius's father had just passed away. Sylvia, our little baby girl was about eight months old at the time. We got her formula, diapers and all we needed and drove straight to San Antonio to be with his mother in this time of loss. It was a long trip. We only stopped for gas so we could get there as soon as possible.

Another memory I want to share is that of so many years of being with my wonderful husband Julius. We have been married for fifty-seven years and are still so happy. Someone at church asked me the other day how we stayed married so long? I told her, you might not believe this but, it is true. My husband and I have never argued. Even when our children were growing up we taught them to live the same way. We would have meetings every Friday evening at the table. We would tell our children to say whatever they needed to share with each other. We taught them the importance of never having hard feelings against each other. We didn't let our kids yell and scream at each other. We didn't do it and we didn't want them to be that way either. We learned from our parents and knew from the beginning that children learn from example. We are grateful for these fifty-seven years we have lived in love together and treasure our values and the values we see growing in our children, grandchildren and great-grandchildren. They add dearly to new memories we are cherishing.

"Train up a child in the way he should go, And when he is old he will not depart from it."
(Proverbs: 22:6)

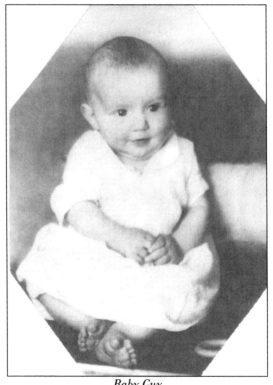

Baby Guy

Birthday Blessing

– Guy Worsham

My daddy had to have been a very loving and brave man who kept his faith amidst real heart-ache. The times were already difficult because he was trying to do his best during the Depression. He definitely wanted a family and must have stormed Heaven to bless him. I know this because my mother was daddy's fourth wife.

Daddy's first wife had a baby and when the baby was born, both the baby and the mother passed away. Again, he married. His second wife became pregnant and when the baby was born, both of them died, too. Daddy married a third wife.

They had a son together, but when the baby was born, this new wife, his third love, passed away. Even though this baby boy lived, how sad my father must have been to lose another wife.

My daddy, Simmie Christian Worsham, never gave up on love. God heard his prayers and honored him when he met my mother Mary Margarete. They married and God blessed their marriage with three boys and one girl. Daddy and mother also loved and cared for his first son, my step-brother from his third wife. So, my mother and daddy did not lack for children and more than likely, were surprised when I came along.

Mother was forty and my father was forty-seven when I was born. Times were very hard because I came during the midst of the Depression. My parents' age and the hardships of the times suggest that I probably was not a planned baby. I believe I was an "uh oh!" to these good Christian parents.

Today, I am eighty-two years young and I would like to share with you what happened on one cold Sunday morning in the month of November. The year was 1930. It was the 16th day of the month. On this particular Sunday our house was the one offered for worship. In those days we really didn't have money to buy gas to drive to the city church. So, we all had church in each other's homes. On this particular Sunday, the blessing had fallen to the Worsham family.

My family had just finished the Sunday service and my mother was ready to deliver her baby. She started having labor pains and the mid-wife was with her. Everyone else was waiting expecting to hear if she had a boy or a girl. Sure enough after a little while the mid-wife came to the door and said, "Folks, it's a little boy. But, I have sad news. He is stillborn." My father's heart must have been crushed.

My sister Wannie Ophelia, at the age of sixteen was already serving the Lord conducting a church service near our home. She received this news and immediately called the people in her service together bombarding heaven in prayer for me. The prayers of these dear saints touched Heaven. God looked down, I believe, and said, "I'll just honor this prayer and put life back into that baby." And that's exactly what happened. After minutes of working with me, trying to restore me back to life, a hearty cry came from my little lungs and all Heaven broke loose in that farmhouse as far back in the country as you can get. God had spared my life for His honor and I give Him the glory always.

"Be anxious for nothing, but in everything by prayer and supplication, with thanksgiving, let your request be known to God."
(Philippians 4:6)

Closing Thoughts

— Paulette Camnetar Meeks

I f you are living with or caring for an older person like the contributors of the stories in this book, what an awesome privilege and responsibility you have! Your reward may not be great in this world. Do not be concerned, for God Who rewards richly, will reward you. Because of your love and care, you will be in the memories they cherish and God our Father will see you in their smiling eyes when

He calls each of them Home. You can be sure God's reward will be beyond imagination for He promises, "And the King will answer and say to them, 'Assuredly, I say to you, Inasmuch as you did it to one of the least of these My brethren, you did it to Me.'" (Matthew 25:40) You will be able to respond in gratitude for those older friends whose stories you've heard and not heard and even the angels will smile as you get to say, "Yes, Lord, I've **been there** and **done that, really!**"

In Search bar :

Paulette Meeks

Amazon.com

Christian books.com

Barnes + Noble.com

CPSIA information can be obtained at www.ICGtesting.com
Printed in the USA
LVOW07s0328080915

453222LV00001B/1/P